mind DOODLES

THIS IS WHAT I KNOW

An unpacking of tricky, raw and lively thoughts

TREENA INNES

www.firstchoicebooks.ca
Victoria, BC

Copyright ©2020 Treena Innes

All rights reserved. No part of this publication may be reproduced, stored in a retrieval system or transmitted in any form or by any means – electronic, mechanical, photocopying, and recording or otherwise – without the prior written permission of the author, except for brief passages quoted by a reviewer in a newspaper or magazine. To perform any of the above is an infringement of copyright law.

Edited by Sylvia Taylor, Sylvia Taylor Communications

Book layout and cover design by Jenny Engwer, First Choice Books

Digital design by Amy Pridday

Artwork by Lori Graham

ISBN: 978-0-2285-0336-1 (paperback)
ISBN: 978-0-2285-0337-8 (hardcover)

Printed in Canada ♻ on recycled paper

firstchoicebooks.ca
Victoria, BC

10 9 8 7 6 5 4 3 2 1

TICK TOCK IT'S FIFTY O'CLOCK

PREFACE

One of my life mantras is live each day like it's your last—as one day it will be. This is the root of inspiration to writing this book. Well, that and I had "write a book by the time I am 50" in big, bold, red on my bucket list, since I was forty. And I keep hearing the tick-tock sounds in my head. And on top of that, are my kids. And on top of that, it's really for anyone I don't know, who may not have anyone bestowing them with entertaining words of insanity, err, I mean, wisdom.

Bottom line: I kept thinking about my young adult kids—what if I get hit by a bus tomorrow? Will they remember all our deep, purposeful, strategically timed conversations? Who will give them lessons-learned with unconditional love? Who will give them shared moments, vulnerable truth and stories that will guide them through their forks in the road?

Who will make them laugh about life's rollercoaster ride?

Initially, my friends gave me the courage to think about writing. I always wrote summary versions of our girls' getaways, with humour

Mind DOODLES

and crass that made my friends howl and read over and over. I thought this humour and crass writing style would be a perfect combination to a great Chick-Lit novel writing adventure.

However, the Chick-Lit writing journey didn't seem to stick. I have book titles from *Sex in the Suburbs*, to *Living Behind Closed Doors*, with starter chapters that entice and curious character descriptions leaving you wanting more, but I couldn't find any resolve to follow through. Mainly, because I don't have a journalism background and really haven't the faintest idea how to formulate a novel! And ultimately, I discovered I do not have a long writing game, as I bore myself too easily.

However, as the young adult kids in my life start talking about moving out, and in fact, by the time I write this book, have moved out—I figure I can manage a quirky non how-to book on life.

Can't I?

I quickly realized that I really had no idea how to write any type of book. So, I started with setting myself up in my best environment. Being a small-town girl from the West Coast, I knew being near the ocean was my secret power. I rented a remote, summer house on Galiano Island with a great deck overlooking the ocean and a comfy chair. I dusted off ten years worth of written musings and hit the ground, writing. I started typing about funny life stories that had stuck to me over the years. I then took those funny life stories and put my mind to work on all the curiosities that were firing around inside my head about them. Not only did I try to answer my own questions, but I also came up with a lot more.

Writing those quirky thoughts would also turn into my own personal reflections. The words were helping me understand and discover *life angles* that I had not considered before. I didn't want these thoughts to only be mine, so I would rally my friends and family in informal focus groups. Ok, confession, they were really cocktail hours, and I tell you,

I sure did get some great insights. Especially after the vodka from the hard bar started to flow.

As each topic started to flourish, I couldn't stop the ideas from rolling. I have lived and continue to live a lively, energetic, action packed life. I started tracking lists and lists of stories and personal essay ideas that came from all this life living.

Thought after thought were plummeting my way and I couldn't stop them. I write these free-falling thoughts on napkins, type notes at rocket-speed on my laptop or I constantly text myself. This is where the doodling vision came into play. As I was trying to describe how these rapid-fire concepts were coming to me, I visualized someone in thought—and sure enough they were doodling. It made great sense to me to describe the fireworks in my head as *mind doodles*. This is truly what I know.

Enjoy the read, as I am already gearing up the sparks for my second book, *This is What I Don't Know*.

thank you
x 1,000,000

DEDICATIONS

Maddi and Travis, my everything—my highly spirited, contributing young people of this world. Who always challenge me to be better—to be my best, without even knowing it. My tooth fairy wish is that you can hear my voice through this book, feel me through my words and into your heart, always. I will forever be your biggest fan. And yes, I am happy-crying.

Hubby, my fated miracle. To be with a man more than half my life who can stand up to me, match my sharp tongue, be a competitor when I need one and trust with my life—I am beyond grateful. You can start collecting on what I owe you on those book-spell-and-grammar-checking late nights, when you are trying hard to be retired.

Who knew writing a book would be so much fun? I think **Sylvia Taylor**, The Great Book Whisperer, knew how much fun it would be, when she agreed to be my writing coach and editor. Sylvia, thank you for matching my life zest, spiciness and making the book magic happen.

Lori Graham, a woman who I can only describe as a true classic—one of the good ones. Your smarts, your caring values and your quiet

Mind DOODLES

observations lead to creativity brilliance. Thank you for being brave and willing to jump into the *unknown*. You are one of the few that can take my whiteboard chicken-scratch vision and turn it into a beautiful masterpiece. Three cheers for your doodling!

My **Focus Group Posse**—you did an outstanding job of peeling back the onion layers while drinking copious amounts of cocktails, challenging the quirky thoughts and supplying an abundance of twisty mind doodles, making me want to come back for more. Until the next one, my lovelies!

To **all my Tribe**, thank you for bringing your full and rich personalities to my world. Without these goodies, this book would not have been born.

TABLE OF Contents

Embrace Weird	1
Perception Distortion	5
Party Like a Rock Star	9
Work Harder, Play Hardest	17
Eyeball Rolling into Legacy	27
Know Your Elements	33
Unconditional Giving	37
Girl vs Boy Sex Talk	43
The "C" Word	47
Losing Your Biggest Fans	53
Bucket List: Write Then Strike That Shit Off	61
Go Play	67
The Friendship Web	71
Get Outside Your Bubble	76
The Stranger Connection	81
Mentor Land	87
Thought Shoot Out	91
1970s Babes	93
Crossing Your Fun Line	97
Decade Mania	99
Parent Joy Ride	103
Natural Highs	107

Mind Doodles

THIS IS WHAT I KNOW

EMBRACE
Weird

Picture your mind full of varying greys, mute tones of beige and goldish browns, perhaps some soft creams—sounds nice and safe, and what? Did I hear? Yes, that's right, BORING!

Now picture vivid hot pinks, blood-vicious reds, blinding bright purples, popping glowing oranges and strips of happy yellows.

That is what weird can bring into your world.

Weird can be simply defined as not conforming in a square. A beautiful thing, really.

Taking us all back to high school: the Preps, the Skids, the Nerds, the Populars, the Feminists, the Rockers, Under the Radar, the Emo, the Punks, the Jocks, the Stoners—whatever group you fell in or out of—everyone knew who the Weirdos were and we avoided them like they were contagious. When you become a grown up, all those high school classifications are wiped clean from the slate. I am talking no crumbs left on the table.

The Jocks could become unemployed boozers. The Nerds, billionaire philanthropists. The Emos, solving world peace. You get the idea.

So, what happens to the Weirdos?

Well, let me tell you. They are the people that grew up and became the interesting ones at lame dinner parties. They offer diversity

Mind DOODLES

in thinking, they are playful, have the most unique careers, contribute their time in entertaining ways, surprise you with their actions and turn ordinary into not so ordinary. They bring the colour!

The best trait of being weird is self confidence. Being completely comfortable with who you are. Knowing you may 'scare' a few non-embracing people away while being a magnet for those that get it. The Weirdos know that the people they draw to them will be well worth the time, and the ones they scare away—well, see ya.

The best thing about Weirdos is the surprise! If you have a relationship with a Weirdo, it's like a wind-up Jack in the Box— a surprise could pop up at any moment. Unexpected, yet welcome. It could be as simple as a surprise on some part of their outfit (I have seen some pretty interesting accessories). It could be a surprise belief or a surprise action. Surprise anything really!

Some of my best times have been with Weirdos, and yes, I am part of the Weirdo tribe, if you are reading this book and don't personally know me. If there are Weirdos in the house on a Saturday night on any dance floor, I can pick them out from across the room with their funky, self-assured dance moves. Perhaps out of rhythm, or bringing back a move from the 80s like The Robot (okay, I admit, that is my own best dance move) and having the time of their lives with a group that is embracing the weird, or rocking it out solo on the floor to their own beat.

Weirdos have the best commentary. One-liners out of nowhere that make sense only to a select few. Their views on life bits and pieces can be a little off colour or a wee bit warped. And their appreciation for the smallest action can be over the top as they can see life in that technicolour layer.

I came to this Weirdo Aha! moment in my early forties. I met this woman, also in her early forties, who I instantly liked and was drawn to. Her high energy was straight shooting, engaging, dynamic and strong. We immediately became friends, and I looked forward to every conversation we had together. Her views were unlike mine, her life appreciation wild and free yet with boundaries. She had some interesting hobbies that have to remain top secret and we sure did make each other laugh. One day we were talking about social circles. She explained she didn't have a friend "tribe." Meaning, a regular group of friends who she would invite to her birthday party or get together at the pub. She claimed she was a Weirdo. For a split second, I felt a negative feeling about her confession and by some miracle, I embraced what I heard. I learned that's what was so special about Weirdos: they live their best lives how they want it and refuse to accept judgement. My new awesome friend was a Weirdo, and I liked her even more because of it!

Something happens around midlife (or, let's face it, anytime in your life) where you can fall into a rut. Day in and day out, to work or school. Routine after routine. Days all start blending into one. Survival, at its best. And how many times have I heard about the cliché mid-life crisis or losing yourself? Well, it is very real.

It could be when responsibility hits, with mortgage, car payments, ongoing demands of kids, keeping a long-term relationship together after years and years and sleeping in the same bed. That 'white picket fence' outside the house can get a little weathered.

It could be anytime in life, where you are headed in a certain direction with school, career or a relationship, and then wham—after time you wonder how you got there, and if this is truly the direction you should be headed.

And I know we have all thought that would never happen to us…but somehow it just does.

So…let the Weirdos be the welcome in your day. In your life. In your space.

They bring that colour to the rut days and times. The weirdos are consistent in their diverse, colourful views, never letting you down.

Mind DOODLES

Embrace the Weirdos! Enjoy the belly laughs, the intriguing conversations, learning from their curious views, and most importantly, thank them for staying weird.

PERCEPTION
Distortion

It seems to come to me in threes. I discover, time to time, that I misjudge the value I am bringing to the table. And not only does this realization blossom once, but back-to-back-to-back. Maybe the three-peat happens because I am shocked into awareness by this perception distortion and start to over-think where else this is happening in my life. You will be happy to know, that after that three-time hit, I do circle back into my reality—which is a much better space to be in.

Let me explain.

Once upon a time (and no, this is no fairy tale) I was a loyal three-year member of this very elite personal training gym. And not only was it elite because they said so, there was also proof in the over-the-top annual fees I paid. I was part of the morning crew and the personal trainers made me feel like a gold medal power-lifting champ! Middle-aged suburb Mom going pro—I was cheered on daily by the gym and also by my morning crew who all felt like family. My gold strength was written up in their bragging monthly newsletters, their savvy social media and proudly talked about by all their staff. I felt part of something big, about something important.

Out of nowhere, the gym decided to move. The move added about twenty more minutes each way to my drive in the morning. Now that does not seem like a big deal, but when you are committed to waking

Mind DOODLES

up at 5:15 am every morning to zoom to your gym training, and then zoom home to get ready for work, and then zoom to get to your first work meeting—that additional forty minutes in your day doesn't begin to work very well. Due to the move, I found myself going to my gym training times a little less.

Because I felt so valued and assumed my loyalty along with my dedication over the past three years was meaningful, I talked to the owner about renegotiating my huge membership fees. I spent time doing a cost analysis and presented the rate I felt I should be paying, based on the unexpected move. I did this figuring generously and with respect, as I know there are many costs to running a business.

So off I went to present my request, and hit a big wall of "ummm, no." Okay, so maybe I had to pump up my case. I counter-backed with my years of dedication, the enormous spirit and encouragement I bring to my morning crew members, plus the fact that I had brought new memberships to the gym.

And still, "ummm, no." I pulled the community leader card. Still "ummm, no."

I sat with this "ummm, no" for awhile. It wasn't the "ummm, no" that was hitting me hard (and yes, I don't like anyone saying no to me) but it was the fact that the value I thought I was providing was actually not the case. Perception distortion all the way. And it was deep.

Did it hurt? Oh yeah.

But was I really to blame? Was the company to blame for misleading me? I thought about ego, about wanting to feel something so bad that maybe I made it up in my head. I thought about all the communication I may have taken out of context, to get to my perception distortion.

And you are probably wondering what were the other two back-to-back life perception distortions that followed. The second one was something at work, and the third one was around a friendship.

But here is the thing: It doesn't really matter, and that's what I have worked through.

My feelings were my feelings. How could that be wrong? Even misjudged, that is how I felt. That is how I was made to feel. And I sure did enjoy those good feelings while they lasted.

And sometimes, well maybe even most of the times, perception can be bang on. And when that happens—look out: fireworks, energy, worlds aligning, things make sense and the world definitely is a better place.

A friendly warning: sometimes these feelings may not be good. After sharing my story and journey to many, I learned that "Imposter Syndrome" is a real thing. It is the experience of feeling like a phony, that gets combined with a lot of internal self doubt. Many people I connected with have felt this syndrome at times of their lives, and many still do, regularly. It can be shocking, jarring and humbling.

I received many common stories of this happening in the workplace. Professionals who are skilled and trained in their expertise have self-doubt creeping into their head and heart, wondering if they really are the right person for the job. Questioning their ability, even though they are fully equipped and knowledgeable for the work. Many shared that it is how you see yourself—if you see yourself as distorted, then who is right? You? Or the person across from you, seeing you?

From this perception distortion journey, I have one big wish.

My big wish for the world is that you find your way to having way more good perception distortion feelings than not-so-good ones.

Cuz those good feelings sure do feel, well, good.

PARTY LIKE A
Rock Star

Now how do I start this one?

It seems I have been living my life like one big party. No, really. Everything, in fact, is one gigantic celebration. And on top of that, when a celebration is truly due, I then take it up a party notch—like a party for the party.

What do these parties look like, you ask?

Well, they can be large, with balloons (well, not balloons, as I actually don't like them) and lots of people dancing with red party cups. Or they can be small, intimate affairs over a nice dinner, or they can be done just one-on-one, well, anywhere, really. They can be impromptu (I can't count the number of living room jump-on-the couch dance parties that have popped up) or they can be planned months in advance.

There really is no definition for how a party is to look. It's all about the celebration intent and the moments.

The celebration intent can also be random. And definitely, the traditional parties such as birthdays

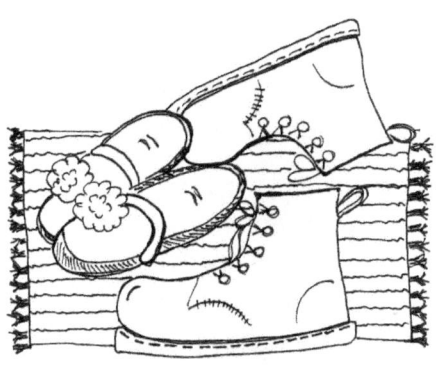

Mind DOODLES

and anniversaries still stand strong. My favourite is when I threw myself an "I am Not 40 Yet" birthday bash, inviting all my over-forty friends to rub it in. Oh, and can't forget the friend who created a flash mob dance for the birthday girl at one party—that was extra awesome. Holiday parties (we love our traditional life-long friend gatherings, bringing together our young adult kids to hang with their friend cousins), house warmings, stags, graduations, divorce parties (had a Silly String fight at that one), baby showers, weddings, graduations, retirements and such, but at times it can just be everyday life. Celebrating living one more day, just because. Throwing a party for a friend you have not seen for awhile and making them the guest of honour.

And I don't think it is just me. For example, who came up with the Ugly Christmas Sweater party? A party lover for sure. I sure wish I would have thought of that one!

What about yacht parties? Ever been on a party boat celebration, just because the sun is out? I had a friend who threw her back out before getting to one of our boat parties. Did that stop her? Heck, no. We had a dance party on the bow of the deck, putting her right in the middle, lying on her back the entire time, as we danced around her. Toga parties! Seriously, who nailed that one? Romans? Greeks? John Belushi? Music festivals, carnivals, concerts (and the pre-party in the hotel, especially getting dressed in the matching sexy outfits to honour the band or singer!)—all parties. I went to my first Foam Party at a pool in Mexico a few years back. Foam was being torpedoed out of cannons at all the poolside guests—now that was a party.

What about Oktoberfest? Hecka party. Gay Pride, St Patrick's Day, Greek Days, Mardis Gras—party, party, party and party. What about in the bleacher bum section at a ball game, tailgate parties in the parking lot cooking up hot dogs on your hibachi before a big game? We all know about Super Bowl parties. The sport party list is long.

And why not?

Sometimes I can be party-prepping and planning back-to-back all year long. It lifts my spirit knowing these celebration occasions are coming together. One of my best friends gets so excited about parties, she asks me for weekly guest updates so she can get even more excited about who she will be hanging with. Many of my friends will start a big banter chat on the pre-party festivities for some playful fun, and you can be sure there is a good amount of post-party banter chat. One of my friends has taken the post-banter to another level and does a play by play on the festivities as a recap in writing, which has us all doing another round of belly laughs. Trust me, you can't buy this entertainment anywhere.

Now, the trick is to find the circles who embrace parties and celebrations of all kinds. I have my "yes" crew that I know will be game for anything and don't even ask me any details of the invite (I love you! You are my favourites.) And then I have my "most likely" crew, who come out to the majority of the celebrations, needing some details for their decision. I do realize not all my celebration styles are everyone's gig. And then I have my "I will think about it" crew, who, if they do decide to come out once or twice a year, are full-on there in party spirit and well worth the wait. And then I have my "on-the-cusp" party crew. They get invited to their first party, as they are showing party potential and maybe invited to a second. Sometimes they return once in a while, sometimes I don't see them for years at a time, and then maybe they don't show up at all. If you see the party spark in someone, you always have to give it a go!

Really, it is about the human connection, before, during and after party celebrations. And if you are wondering, it is not all wrapped around cocktails and glitter.

One of my favourite celebrations was for my mom and dad when they passed away. My parents were not big party goers (seems I

Mind DOODLES

have done some rebelling here) and did not want the typical funeral or end of life celebrations. So, we decided to celebrate in an intimate, meaningful way. We honoured a family tradition of piling in the truck with our cooler stocked, going down a dirt road, finding a rushing river with a good place for a fire and having a wienie roast. So, dressing up in our Sunday sweat pant finest, we pulled out the blue cooler (it used to be orange from the 70s) and loaded it up with our traditional stock of cream soda, orange crush, hot dogs, marshmallows, potato salad, piggy puffs and popcorn twists. As we sat around the fire, we celebrated mom and dad's memory, with many storytelling laughs and tears—having our own kind of party without the glitter.

A top birthday party moment was when one of my best friends turned fifty. This is the friend I was talking about earlier that requests the weekly guest updates, so her birthday party had to be something extra, extra WOW. We decided to have a parade in her honour—yup, you heard right, and we even surprised her. I still remember that celebration moment—her driving around the corner and up the street (thinking we were going for a bike ride) and forty of her favourite women dressed in their party outfits; all wearing matching pink camouflage visors imprinted with a message; a big birthday banner leading at the front; an old-school boom box playing our fave AC/DC T.N.T. tune marching down the street towards our friend, singing at the top of our lungs. A parade celebration success!

One of my warmest celebrations was a Work Partner Appreciation party. Our organization brought together all the people in our community who have supported our vision and mission success. We tasked our leadership to speak from the heart on the impact the supporters have made on them personally, as well as their profession. I had the honour to emcee the party and could see from the front of the room, all the guests' faces and expressions of gratitude, as they heard the heartfelt words spoken to them. I also saw the enormous appreciation flowing from the speakers, in an authentic way, as it was unscripted. Those moments will always warm my heart.

We do a lot of celebrating in our back yard. And a lot of celebrating in our kitchen. When my husband and I bought our family home, our vision was to have a party house along with throwing in a tire swing for the kids.

Our kids grew up with celebrations going into the wee hours of the morning with a lot of 'loud' and they could sleep through anything. The party continues in the morning, when the smell of coffee brews and the sleepover guests wake up. Big pancake breaky hits the table, and more celebration. It has become part of our family culture. In fact, even with the kids moved out, they still 'borrow' our home for the night for their parties. I am still whipping up party appetizers for the young adults and my husband hits the margarita machine as the bartender. Yup, pancake breaky always follows, and those young adults sure can feast in the morning on little sleep.

Our family home has seen beautiful back yard long-table dinner parties under the stars with grandparents, neighbours, young friends, lifelong friends and connections, celebrating together. Our hot tub, complete with disco party lights, has its own party theme from time to time. Our yard has been a venue for anyone who needs to celebrate, and I have seen it go from West Coast forest to Japanese lanterns blowing in the wind looking like a fairy tale. Our home also hosts many work parties, and, in the end, it is always a kitchen party. We even had a party called "Perogie Fest"—250 perogies made and devoured with garlic sausage (only two menu items on the buffet)—we celebrated perogies! Our annual summer BBQ celebrating "Happy Summer" is a fan favourite, and the most outrageous party our home has seen is the "blond versus brunette" chick party.

Huh?

Mind DOODLES

This one is even hard for me to explain, and I have no idea how that transpired, with the exception of just celebrating good, crazy fun.

Every few years (or so) my friends and I rally our Tribes out on a warm summer Saturday night. We split the guests into two teams: blondes and should-be blondes versus the brunettes. The first task is to get each team to choose a captain, which takes a good hour as part of the never-met-before bonding. Then the Party Masters (myself and the excited best friend) explain the games and point system. Then we show off the trophy for competitive inspiration. The games can be anything from smashing through a pinata, to a trampoline dance-off, to a scavenger hunt. Yes, this is the g-rated game version explanation. And there is always a grand finale game that can take you from losing to winning. Winner takes home goodie bags, bragging rights and the gold trophy. But most of all, it's a bunch of people coming together, half of them never meeting before, and celebrating fun. Some say it's the funnest party they have ever been to, and requests come in regularly to book the next one!

I hope I have party-inspired, or at the very least, encouraged you to say Yes to your next celebration invite knowing how rewarding it is to have these entertaining connections in your life.

Now off to planning our Tiki Hut Bar opening bash this year. Now, that will be a good party!

WORK HARDER, Play Hardest

I grew up with a strong force of work ethic. And I really do mean strong, as in superhuman strength.

Dad was a blue-collar worker who worked two jobs, including a day shift and a night shift, so Mom could take on the job of fulltime Mom and not have to work outside the home.

I watched my dad get up early each day, put on his steel-toe work boots while Mom, in her baby blue housecoat, hair rollers and fuzzy slippers, filled Dad's thermos with hot coffee and packed his sturdy black lunch kit with white bread and mustard bologna sandwiches.

Dad came home every night promptly at 5:00 pm for dinner. I saw Mom pride herself on having a delicious roast beef and spud dinner complete with green peas from the garden plus glasses of perfectly cold milk for the family ready, precisely, at 5:00 pm. And let me tell you, could that woman yell across the neighbourhood from the back deck to my brother and I, to get home for dinner on time. Yup, we ran. Maybe even sprinted. We all had our "chair" at the dining room table, and no one dared to shake it up. Family stability at its best.

Then the after-dinner turnaround happened: another sturdy black lunch kit got organized for what I assume were late night snacks and off went Dad for the nightshift. Mom took her

Mind DOODLES

Mom job seriously and did it with great excellence. She was a master cleaner, and you could eat off the floor. She led the family dynamics in her station wagon, like the CEO of a large bank that she could have been. Sewing Halloween costumes, baking cakes for the school cake walk (and could she make a mean poppy seed chiffon!), sports chauffer, our own bologna sandwich lunch kits complete with Ding Dongs, home-made jams, dentist appointments, canning, vegetable garden growing, chief craft-maker, and all around good helping neighbour. Seems she was always watering the neighbours' plants while they were on holidays or swapping baked goods. Mom showed us what being a good neighbour means and how important it was for all the neighbours to take care of each other.

I learned later in life that Mom had a dream of becoming a nurse, but she explained that her CEO-of-the-Home role was more than enough dream for her. What a woman.

Day in and day out, this work/life happened, until Dad's days off. Then it was a day of rest. Well, from a kid perspective it looked that way, but maybe not so much for Dad. It meant family Snakes and Ladders games, asking Dad to come outside and play catch with me—even as a kid, I could tell he was pooped out and negotiating time with me for a nap in between.

But the absolute best was when I knew Dad worked extra shifts and came home with "meal tickets" to the local burger drive-in. He would walk in with the tickets in the front breast pocket of his work shirt and pull them out to proudly show us all. Now that was a treat for everyone about once a month—piling in the station wagon and heading to the drive-in for our favourite milkshakes. Five o'clock roast beef and potato dinner was off the menu!

The Big Kahuna treat was how my parents scrimped and saved their pennies (and probably back then it literally was pennies), and if you don't know what a penny is when you read this, please Google it. Sigh.

Anyways, we hopped on the first plane ride of our lives and went to Disneyland! You can imagine this was a big, big thing, as our typical family vacation was an annual road trip in that same reliable station wagon, driving for fifteen hours straight, windows partially open and the car filled with cigarette smoke, to a farm in Alberta to see my grandma, aunts, uncles and cousins. Which we did love doing every year. But, we did hit the extra-jackpot with this one-time family trip to see Mickey Mouse!

I recognized my parents' hard-work ethic to pull this together for our family at a young age. It was standard practice to always prioritize work first, and then get to the good stuff. It was common language to hear, "I have to work," which meant all else got put on hold.

The message was clear: work was a means to living and having the life you wanted.

On this work-ethic learning journey, our lives got turned upside down when I was a teenager. Dad suddenly lost his electrician job. It was hard to understand why a man who was so dedicated and worked so hard for a company could, poof, just end. As a teenager, it felt like life as we knew it got hit by the 'pause button.' No more day and night sturdy black thermos packing for Dad and no more drive-in meal ticket burger treats.

But you guessed it, the meat and potato dinner was still game-on for 5:00 pm each night! I saw Mom rise to her CEO-of-the-Home role with passion and determination. I saw her let Dad feel sorry for himself with a whisky in his hand each day, but not for long. I saw her use her greatest negotiation and strategic skills to get Dad out of bed, out of the house, and then out of nowhere, they bought a struggling delicatessen and turned it around after five years.

I saw a new work ethic emerge. One of those "pull up your bootstraps and get on with it" extreme efforts splashed with a huge dash of risk. My parents, who never owned a business before, let alone work

Mind DOODLES

together as business partners, took a small shop deli battling for sales and turned it into an expanded European speciality food and lunch café. This is where I discovered Jägermeister, a stomach bitter from Germany, that was legally sold in the deli, before the days of it being a popular shot drink at the nightclub. Okay, that's for another book.

There were long work hours with expansions into catering, as Mom took her Ukrainian kitchen talents to a new level with Dad using his newly discovered business skills. Dad poured over the books each night with his cigarette smoke billowing above his head, figuring out the most profitable revenue streams. My parents hard work came to fruition as they sold the deli for a healthy profit so they could both retire modestly to their backyard fruit trees and tend to their gardens. I continued to see that work ethic through their golden years as they dug, pruned, planted, weeded, tamed, picked and worked in their dirt, reaping their food rewards—eating and living off their land.

These work-ethic life lessons have taught me well, along with adding my own tweaks. I believe work can be viewed from a variety of angles.

But before I get into that...I am firm that the number one priority in this work harder-play hardest attitude is the play part. Work to play—making sure you are in a work environment that encourages you to work/life balance and live life outside the work walls. If you are getting pumped up, skip to the topic on "Go Play"!

Back to the variety of work angles.

You can work for your own pleasure and satisfaction finding work that is your passion. It may not have the healthy cash return (or no return at all if you wish for the CEO-of-the-home role) but know you will hop out of bed each morning wanting to get at the day. That can be pretty priceless.

You can work for the end game of money. Maybe not fully being rewarded by the work, but it is a means to an end, with your paycheque paying for your joys in life, or to achieve a specific life goal, or simply to pay your rent.

You can work as a steppingstone for the greater good of your career or your life. It could be an interim job where you need experience in order to get to the next job level. It could be a job in another city, where you need connections, or maybe a temporary stop in your life before the next journey.

Personally, I think you will hit the ultimate motherload if you can find work that is your passion and meets your financial goals. Can you imagine loving what you do, jumping out of the bed to get at it, and have the financial means to achieve what your vision is outside of your work hours? The big win is finding a work environment that you can connect with as your "work family." Now imagine hopping out of bed, being happy with your paycheque that lands in your bank account and adoring the people you create your work magic with.

Believe me, it can happen.

With all the above and beyond work ethics I grew up with, I have had a good baseline to figure this out.

As a kid, I hit the ground running with work as I liked money and buying what I wanted. My first job was a cleaning job on Saturdays and selling Avon door to door. Talk about developing cleaning and selling skills at an early age. If you must know, I sure do hate cleaning and sure do love selling. Well, we call it storytelling these days. I worked with a novel writer, organizing her chaos. I worked in a hair salon booking appointments, washing hair and learned all about gossiping. I worked in our famous family European deli named Deli-icious—how adorable is that? I ate and snuck my friends way too many black forest ham and swiss cheese submarine sandwiches, probably losing money for the deli each Sunday I worked.

I moved to the remote part of an island where I discovered hippies and surfers. I worked three jobs 'round the clock, managing a whale

Mind DOODLES

museum (yup, that is what I said) where the hippie owners called me on Day 3 of my new job to let me know they would be in jail for a few weeks, as the police had arrested them for chaining themselves to a tree—and did I have any management experience? I worked for a whale watching tour company (more sales), was a waitress and hotel front desk clerk. Oh, did I tell you I lived in a small closet in the back of that whale museum? Nights were a little freaky with all those whale bones close by.

I moved to the Big City at eighteen years old and got my first "real" job at a bank! I arrived in the city, suitcase in hand, finally finding the bank through the busy streets, and went to organize my student loan. Signing my papers, the loan lady asked me if I wanted a job on a Saturday as a statement filing clerk while I went to school full time. Heck yeah, I did. Somehow the city sucked me into all the glitz, parties and shiny fun, and stole my work ethics. By Month 2 at the bank, I got sat down by the most serious Scottish lady who straight-up told me that if I wanted to keep my one day a week Saturday job, that I in fact had to show up to work on Saturdays. Doh, right! The reminder was actually helpful—I was back on the work ethic train!

The bank was my first experience as a "work family." Drinks after work at the local pub, potlucks and friends. I even met my future husband while filing all those bank statements. From there it was on to Accounting Land with companies that also promoted "work family" and where I met brilliant mentors and lifelong, caring friends.

I learned about corporate politics and watched my work role models graciously manage corporate take-overs and buy-outs. I experienced department differences—sales versus accounting versus service. I witnessed leadership gracefully maneuver through each department's demands and needs. I was part of the start-up and dot-com riches plus the busts. I was supposed to be a billionaire, instead of using my shareholder documents for wallpaper. I saw how money caused trust to break, ruin relationships, and bring out the vicious horns of greed. I saw how pressure changed people, some for the good and some for the not so good. I saw the blossom of culture, and I saw it break.

I had the honour to take all the corporate learnings to the charitable world. I learned about transitioning business culture to non-profit culture, and how aligned the two worlds are. I learned the power of volunteers investing their time to accomplish big feats. I saw everyday people in leadership roles making significant change to help people with no expectations of a personal gain. I have worked with powerful staff teams that give their all to achieve the greater good. I saw the rare beauty of modesty and the herculean strength of commitment.

I started to really learn about work culture, and how important this is to match your own culture and expectations in the workplace. I also observed that you need to keep an eye on it, in case it shifts and changes—no longer being a happy match.

I learned that with every job or organization I considered or interviewed for, that I was getting better and better at understanding the work culture each provided and if we would potentially be a match. I learned that I would not accept a job if the culture was not aligned, and I would fight hard for jobs where I saw it could. I also learned that I didn't always get it right, and sometimes had to make quick job exits.

When I grew up to be the boss, I knew I wanted to inspire my workplaces to make culture a Number One priority, and to name it, live it, breathe it and be accountable to it. I knew I wanted to find people to become my "work family" who also wanted to build culture values, whether they knew it or not. I also find myself as a consumer, seeking businesses that also carry the "work family" cultures and similar ethics. Sadly, this is getting tougher and tougher to find.

This culture list carries the same attributes year after year, but sure does grow as the work world learns and grows itself. Work/life balance, transparency, flexibility, having a positive outlook and humour in the

Mind DOODLES

workplace, creates a consistent foundation. Peer empowerment, taking time to celebrate, recognition, self-direction, giving permission to take cues from each other when we are working too much, non-judgemental attitudes and openness to challenge each other, are all part of the growing culture list.

Bottom line: whatever work dynamic you belong to, just keep figuring it out and moving forward. We know that work, whether paid or unpaid, takes up a significant part of our week. Make it good for yourself and know that you need confidence to make the change that is best for you, with your passion or productivity. Don't hang around too long in a workplace that is not jiving with you. Give it enough time to know, but not too much time, or bitterness may creep in, or your confidence gets knocked down and it becomes tougher to say goodbye.

There are endless opportunities waiting for you—find them, grab them, so you can work harder and play hardest.

EYEBALL ROLLING INTO *Legacy*

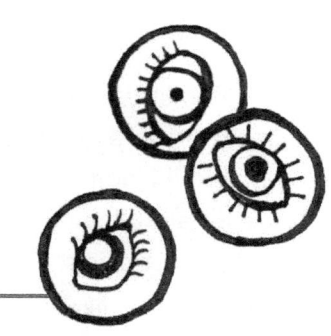

I imagine after flipping through this book, you can see how I get a lot of eyeball rolling directed my way. You must know, I welcome a good eyeball roll. I sure like to give them, and I absolutely love to receive them. In fact, I think I have mastered the eyeball roll. Pause, get the face expression completely blank, raise the left eyebrow, set your eyes deeply to the back of your head, let 'er roll left to right and add a right cheek-lift-smirk for completion. A head shake could also be added as a signature bonus. So, you are probably wondering what an eyeball roll has to do with legacy. Stick with it, you will find out shortly.

The eyeball roll variety is endless. Sometimes they are ever so slight that you second guess if you actually did an eyeball roll or if it was all in your head. I call this the Eyeball Roll Ghost. It's for those split-second reactions that you quickly want to pull back or find yourself unsure in your thoughts. Then there is the Eyeball Roll Beast that is full of big passion and a big punch in your gut emotion. Oh yeah, this one is good. Likely a result of something you vehemently disagree with or you may be reacting to the person delivering a message thinking they really don't know what they are talking about. The

Mind DOODLES

Eyeball Roll Beast is long, it's deep, and quite frankly, can physically hurt your eyes. The eyeball roll assortment wouldn't be complete without the Eyeball Roll Habit. Yes, I am talking to all of you, as you know you do it. The eyeball roll that just comes so naturally, without thought, without feeling, it just exists. Sometimes without any reason, like an eye twitch.

The reason I like to receive eyeball rolls of any variety, really, is that I know you are listening. Whether you want to or not, whether you agree or not, you are hearing me! One point for me! The champions of eyeball rolls have been, hands down, from my husband and kids. However, now that I think about it, I do have a few friends and colleagues who may be in the running for a close second. As Champion Eyeball Rollers, they all carry the same trait: their eyeball rolls are capital P predictable. Especially the Eyeball Roll Beast variety.

While volunteering for our local community foundation, a foundation member handed out a thank you gift to each of us at one of the meetings for giving our time to the cause. It was a book on legacy giving, written by a local citizen.

Legacy giving can be described as how you will be remembered when you are gone from this world. What mark did you leave? What impact did you make while you were living? What difference did you make for the future? Big stuff, I know.

The book caught my interest not because it was on legacy giving, as I have read a mountain of those over my fundraising career, but because it was written by someone local. As I started to dig into the chapters, it was clear it was a different type of legacy giving. It had a spin. The message was that you didn't have to leave a big building in your name or give away your estate when you die, or build a bridge in your grandmother's honour to create a legacy. The book message was that you could have a "family legacy" that was meaningful to your family, that was as simple as picking up garbage each week. Are you kidding?

I was intrigued! Mainly because our estate will be drained out cash-wise when we die, which will make sense to you when you read the chapter on "Party Like A Rock Star." Plus, I currently do not have enough in my savings account to build a bridge. The booked talked about how there were many meaningful ways to leave a legacy, to leave your footprint, even without big bucks and in your own way.

I liked where this book was going.

The book recommended starting by defining your family values. It explained that the legacy can be wrapped around your values. For example, a small act, such as picking up garbage in your neighbourhood, could be aligned with an environment value and can become your legacy. Well, that sounded too easy. I thought about my own values that I kept accountable to in my relationships, partnerships and myself. I take that seriously and have been known to have classic temper tantrums over it.

I thought about all the values and value statements I have led and participated in over the years in my work environments. Values were always the foundation for good decision making, especially when the decisions were complex and hard. Values also helped in getting the organization back on track, as continuous visits to the values, challenged directions and strategies. All good, positive stuff.

Why not have agreed values in your family unit? I was all in on this idea.

I took the opportunity to rally the family troops on a hike one sunny Sunday afternoon. I brought the book along to work through our values at one of our awesome hiking viewpoint stops, complete with some yummy snacks. Oh yeah, doesn't that sound warm and fuzzy? My kids will tell you that I had to bribe, drag, push, encourage, yell, cry and pull them, on any family hike. And this was no different. You can guarantee I wasn't about to tell them about my legacy-defining values at the viewpoint-yummy-snack plan! They would have ditched the hike for sure.

By some miracle, that day all four of us hiked around a peaceful lake,

Mind DOODLES

ending up looking out at the pretty view. I didn't wait long to bring out the family values exercise and yummy snacks and explain with all my gusto that today was the day we were going to build our family legacy! I am confident that within five seconds of my explanation there were three over-the-top Eyeball Roll Beasts targeted at me and the book. It was like a staged performance of Master Eyeball Rolling wizardry.

I did not let that stop me. In fact, I think it encouraged me! I was determined to name our family values so that we could make our proud legacy footprint. So, with extra human effort of prodding and begging, we decided on twelve values: be honest in life and with each other always; have a strong work ethic; spend quality time together; no family guilting; keep each other laughing; do fun stuff together; earn independence; support each other; work, life, play balance; celebrate each other; respect each other's uniqueness and help each other.

The twelve values came in handy over the years, as I pulled them out when it felt like one of us was heading in a different direction. Yes, more eyeball rolling. I also made extra efforts to review them to see if they were still valid and needed to be refreshed. Again, more eyeball rolling.

The foundation of these values on how we behave, react, share and live our lives together, really did make sense as a good reminder on what we committed to in our family relationships. The values kept us strong when things may have been going sideways in the teenage years, and kept me grounded as a parent, knowing we had these words to lean into when needed.

By now, you are probably waiting to hear what our family legacy is. The big footprint, the big impact we can pass on to our great great grandchildren. Well, funny thing is, we never did come up with our family legacy. Maybe the value exercise was enough? Maybe the family legacy is the values setting and passing on that values-setting torch to the next generation? Maybe it was just exhausting enough getting them together to talk through values, and no energy left for the legacy convo?

Or maybe it's time now to dust off those values and finally put a family legacy into action! And you guessed it—bring on the Eyeball Beast Rolling.

KNOW YOUR
Elements

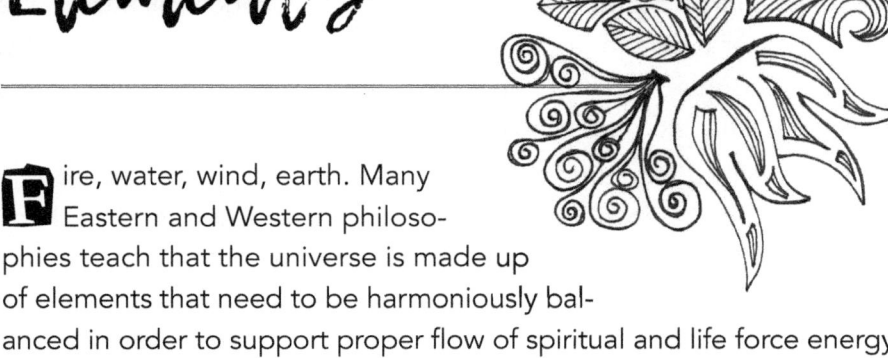

Fire, water, wind, earth. Many Eastern and Western philosophies teach that the universe is made up of elements that need to be harmoniously balanced in order to support proper flow of spiritual and life force energy.

I know, right?

You could spend years studying these philosophies. Fire brings passion, earth brings grounding, water brings balance and wind brings movement. Trust me, the learning goes on and on. But what I'm talking about is using your own instinct and knowing your own distinctive elements to bring you up or bring you down.

For example, I struggle with wearing anything black. It makes me grumpy—and yes, I know it's slimming and this should make me happy. If you opened up my clothing closet door, you would be challenged to find a black item amongst the sea of greens, blues, creams, oranges, greys and reds. I know for myself, wearing colour brightens my energy and black flattens it. And trust me, I try to keep buying that hot little black dress—but it always hits the NO pile at the store, slimming and all.

I also have discovered what environments or regions bring me up or bring me down. Years ago, my

Mind DOODLES

in-laws moved to a very dry climate. The landscape often brown, desert like, tumbleweeds thrown in and the air super dry. When we made the three-hour drive to go visit, by hour two, I started to feel the dryness on my skin; the moisture sucked out of the air and the climate making a major switch. And no, this was not because I was getting closer to the in-laws. I loved their company! Feeling this dry, desert environment change, somehow made me sleepy and restless versus my usual exuberant energy.

I didn't understand it for the longest time, as I know people love those dry, hot environments. So, I would just accommodate those road trips, knowing I wouldn't be at my best and putting up with it. I finally understood it when one of my best friends moved to the very same dry environment. She too would talk about how the dry weather was sucking her soul empty. Yes, that dramatic! When she came home to visit, leaving the dry atmosphere behind, I could see the instant positive change in her energy. We agree, we are both rainforest gals all the way—bring on the gigantic wet-teddy-bear cedar trees!

One of my favourite moments was being with my mom when it was windy. She loved the wind for many reasons. Being a practical woman of nature, she loved drying the laundry in the wind on the clothesline. I can still hear the wind chimes and smell of Fleecy in the air. She loved to put her face in the wind the best. When I watched Mom do this, I could see the composure in her face transform to complete relaxation and a very content smile. When the wind swooshed by her cheeks, she would reflect, "I wonder whose cheeks the wind just touched before mine?" Wind was truly one of her elements.

I also know I am not a cold element kind of gal. I know, I know, not a dry climate gal, not a black clothing gal. Let's just say I am getting clearer on what I like. When fall turns to winter, I know I have to set my mind to hunker down; to use this time to ramp up work, take on a hobby, focus on anything but the cold. The cold makes me not feel well physically. And wearing layers and layers of fluffy, puffy clothing I can barely move my body in, doesn't help.

And believe me I've tried. I have made efforts to embrace the cold and all the fun activities Mother Nature offers. I have tried the Snow Bunny vision a few times, getting ski geared up, grabbing a cute toque and off I go on the swinging gondola to the top of the mountain that awaits my ski talents. However, at the top it starts with a shaky gondola departure, then a smiley picture at the peak with the cold cutting through my fleece scarf, while my lips turn blue. Then I find the run that I'm not sure is even the right one and shocker—my first nosedive tumble into the snow. Yup, freezing. This time, with snow jammed up my nostrils. Nope, not a fan of the cold.

I don't know how all the right elements magically come together, but my roots are definitely West Coast. The remote, rugged, raw, salt in the air ocean; the green, lush, wet earth and gnarly wind-blown trees, makes me feel alive and has some rejuvenating superpower. And I know when I need an injection, or when I have been away from it too long. An internal withering feeling of sorts, happens. I also have the opposite element need: to be in the city—near dynamic life, diversity, people energy, live tunes, sweaty dancing, funky shopping options, good food and oh, those city lights.

I also have an extreme need to just make a Life Exit to a completely different environment and country. An almost element-shake-up craving. As soon as I step off the plane into a new environment, I can feel my body take the three or four days to test and settle into the new elements, deciding if this is going to be a thumbs up or thumbs down.

Your elements don't come in a box, and one size definitely does not fit all. Your feelings and reactions to elements are endless.

Knowing when you need some alone time to regroup is knowing your element. Or when you are craving your Tribe of friends for some goofy belly laughs. How about feeling the need to bring your fami-

Mind DOODLES

ly together around a traditional meal, or a cozy fire complete with a card game of Cheat? Or some sexy time with your partner for some much-needed connection? Volunteering your time and putting yourself in that element can be an incredible high of its own.

We aren't always lucky to be in our elements or have the elements at our fingertips to give us what we need, all the time. But knowing what they are, what we need, is a beauty start. Knowing your elements, using your instincts, filling your cup, lifting your spirit—whatever it is. Listen to it, hear it and enjoy the element ride.

UNCONDITIONAL
Giving

One of my close friend's teenage daughter was inspired to host a fundraiser to support South African young women. My friend has always been a true giver, from her profession to her community to her friends and family. It was no surprise that her daughter started walking in her footsteps. I felt honoured to be asked to do a little speak on philanthropy to the one hundred invited guests at a high tea fundraiser.

Public speaking, or being a keynote speaker, being interviewed on TV, emceeing or presenting in any form has always come very natural and easy to me in front of large groups of people. And in my career, I have spoken countless times at a podium. My biggest crowd was over one thousand, with the Premier of British Columbia there, creating awareness for foster children. I was bold enough to ask those thousand people to close their eyes as I walked them through a journey of a young child in foster care. I think I practiced that one for weeks! And yes, I sighed the biggest relief of a lifetime that it was a success and not slammed as a media joke in the newspaper the next day. Back to the tea fundraiser.

I took my speaking job seriously and started to prepare. What was different about this crowd, was that many were my friends, and most were my acquaintances in our local community. It was not a room full of a thousand

strangers I would never see again, but one hundred people I know and connect with regularly.

I was determined to find a giving topic that would reach their hearts and honour the young woman who put herself out there for this fundraising. I spent a lot of time thinking about how touched I was by her, being a teenager, to give her time so freely when we know how this generation is so caught up in being connected to their technology—and how it seems they are never free. I then spent a lot of time thinking about the older generation that has touched me in my fundraising career, and one woman in particular, who gave me a life lesson on unconditional giving.

I had an Aha! moment and married these two reflections for the presentation topic of Unconditional Giving.

The presentation started with my explanation of unconditional giving, which means giving without personal benefit. No charity influence, no tax receipt, no personal gain, no marketing benefit, no networking, no nothing—only because it's the right thing to do, it fits your values, you want to, and you are able to.

I told the story of my first career 'ask' as a professional fundraiser. I worked for a charity supporting children and youth in a start-up fundraising phase. It was so start-up, that what we needed money for, was paying the electricity bill to keep the lights on! I was introduced to a well-known philanthropist named Edith. I was invited to her home to tell her more about the charity and how we were helping the children. I did my homework and research in the weeks ahead of our meeting, on what dollar amount would be appropriate to ask for. I researched how to make the 'fundraising ask,' when to ask, the type of ask, who to ask, the approach of the ask, the art of the ask—the learning felt endless.

As a sidebar, I worked with a new fundraising team once, who thought I kept saying, "fundraising ass" versus "fundraising ask." That was a good belly laugh. Back to Edith.

After all the Ask homework, the day had come to make the Ask. I dressed in my best asking suit, arrived at Edith's home, and rang the doorbell as my knees knocked and hands sweated with nerves. I was taken by elevator to the top floor of a breathtaking penthouse with sweeping views of English Bay. Stepping into the foyer, I was welcomed by a beautiful black grand piano with pictures of adorable grandchildren and great grandchildren.

I was also warmly welcomed by a woman who was nothing but elegant and lovely, wearing her own beautiful suit. I immediately relaxed and had visions of us talking for hours about her adorable grandchildren as we sat down to tea. Well, one thing you need to know about Edith is that she came from a shrewd background of building successful businesses. There was no talk of the adorable grandchildren at the start of the tea, as the conversation started with her asking why I was there.

As my sweaty hands returned, I lost track of all my 'ask' homework and blurted out that we needed $10,000 to keep the lights on. Edith instantly agreed to the $10,000 but said she wanted the funding to go directly to the children for school supplies or support services they needed. Edith was clear she did not want to pay for the lights.

I was flying high with the $10,000 donation. Yes! And I readily agreed to her request, even though I knew the children were well funded with school supplies and support services at that time. As I took the elevator down from the lovely English Bay penthouse, I was feeling confident that I could fundraise ask with other donors and find funding for the electric bill.

Well, it seemed the fundraising ask research and homework was right—it does take a long time to nurture that fundraising ask to a Yes. The following two weeks I received nothing but No's.

I started to get really worried about keeping our lights on.

Mind DOODLES

Out of nowhere, I received a phone call from Edith. She had called to apologize. I asked for what, as she had just given us the generous gift of $10,000. She explained that she was being selfish, asking the charity to direct the funding towards what she wanted. I *realized*, that Edith *realized* that she was receiving a giving-benefit by visualizing the children receiving school supplies or tutoring services that she had funded. Edith felt it was selfish for her to tell the charity where she thought the money should go, when she should rely on the charity to know where her investment was best needed. Edith said that if we needed the donation to keep the lights on, then that was where it must be used.

This was a true-life lesson in unconditional giving. The impact of that experience awakened me to look at donating in a very different way. In fact, in following years, my unconditional giving experience has continually matured.

One Christmas I was hosting a party, yes, that is a surprise, I know. I asked our friends to not bring flowers or an appetizer or a gift, but instead, to bring money or an item from the list I gave them, to help a family. I set up a big box in my entrance hallway, and when my friends walked in, they happily dropped their donation or item in the box. After the party, the box was overflowing with generosity and my friends really appreciated the giving opportunity. I contacted the local charity I was working with to let them know the wish list had been filled for the family and I pictured myself arriving at the doorstep, playing Santa.

I learned another significant lesson that day. The charity asked me to consider not playing Santa, as the family may feel embarrassed. The charity asked me not to wrap the gifts for the children, as that might be a task the mom wished to do for her kids. The charity asked me to consider buying a gift certificate to the grocery store so the family could do their own turkey dinner shopping together, as a nice family holiday experience. The charity asked me to consider dropping off the donations to their office so we could honour the pride of the family versus me, a stranger, ringing their doorbell.

That charity really helped me think through unconditional giving in a bigger way. The "playing Santa" I wanted to do was for my giving-benefit, so I could see the people I was helping. And, if I admit, it was part of making me feel good about my action. I thought of Edith and truly understood her selfish-giving sentiment. I was understanding more and more, about the donor desire to see the tangible benefit as their giving-reward, versus just giving and walking away.

I continue to be aware of unconditional giving and do my best to make sure it is embedded in my own philanthropy. I do my best to select the charitable organization I am giving to, looking at their credibility, who they are helping, and performance of programs that are making a difference. I push myself to simply give to a charity and have them select the area of greatest need, as long as it aligns with my values. Just like Edith.

I admit, it's not easy, as I love playing Santa, and who wouldn't want to see the tangible reward of their donation? I know unconditional giving for me will be a work in progress. I am also aware that some people just do this easily, without life lessons from Edith or a charity. Like that teenager, who unconditionally put on the fundraiser for women across the world whom she will never meet. Giving of her time, with no benefit.

A great bonus of my High Tea fundraiser presentation that day, was putting together for myself that the Millennials and Generation Z already have unconditional giving figured out. They are being raised surrounded by their education culture and reminded constantly in social media, that it is their responsibility to change the world—and they believe they can, and they will. Because if it fits in your values, it's the right thing to do, if you want to and you are able to.

Thank you, Millennials and Generation Z, for embracing unconditional giving, easily. Future unconditional giving, and the world, is in good hands.

GIRL VS BOY
Sex Talk

Oh yeah, you know it, this is going to be the juicy chapter. Nowhere near R rated, but definitely a good PG-13. I have become aware that it seems whenever my girlfriends are together in conversation, we always hit a discussion on sex. And it can be on anything, without any boundaries or any rules. It has simply become the norm—and why not? Isn't this how we all got here on this planet? Why would you want to keep sex talk top secret these days?

We talk about sexual positions. Which typically sends us into uncontrollable giggling fits for hours. We may physically show each other, after the cocktails start flowing, fully clothed of course. We may learn from each other a new move or a new style. This is truly entertainment you can't buy...err, well, you can buy it, but let's not go there.

We may talk about the lack of sex in our lives, and how to turn the heat up in the bedroom. And it could be the exact opposite: we may talk about the abundance of sex, and why that is happening. Sharing, sharing and more sharing. Also know, we usually come up empty-handed with any good answers. Again, more good entertainment.

We talk about spicing up sexual relationships with outfits, toys, games, sprays and any other antics we have newly discovered. We talk about what gets us motivated in the sex department, what works and what doesn't. We talk about masturbation in the same way.

Mind DOODLES

We talk through with friends who are not in long term sexual relationships and understand "hook ups" or "friends with benefits" and the attraction of them as well as the disdain. For adult girls, there is a big mix of satisfaction and guilt all wrapped in this package, with one crooked red bow to talk through.

We talk about understanding how hard it would be, to be without sex for a long period of time, if hook ups or a long-term sexual partnership are not in the picture, and then try to understand how long-term relationships can evolve without sex while still being solid and happy. We talk about how in a relationship one partner may be friskier than the other, and what that looks like.

The effects on the ego as well as the compromise.

We talk about morning sex, afternoon delights, bedtime sex, oral sex, dining room table sex, shaking it up sex, balcony sex, elevator sex—really, just sex, sex and more sex. Sex is such a great word really. So succinct and sharp.

We talk about the Millennials being over sexualized. Having sex.com at their fingertips on the Internet, when in the old days we had to hide in the corner of 7 Eleven to sneak a peak at the Playgirl magazines. The magazines were always hidden behind a black cloth on the rack behind the fudgsicles and we had to be careful to not get caught. Or we had to work the TV 'rabbit ears' to get it just right between Channel 2 and 3 to catch a "blue" movie glimpse that just showed some skin. Or that rare book you could find at your friend's parents' house. What was that called? *Joys of Sex*? *Debbie Does Dallas*? *Something about Margaret*? Bottom line, risky-business books were limited and challenging to find.

We talk about what this easy access to sex and sometimes inappropriate imaging to our kids will mean. What do they think sex is really like between two lovers when they see intense sexual images and acts on the Internet or TV, that seem to have no restricted ratings these days?

THIS IS WHAT I KNOW

I think I failed in this parenting arena myself, when I tried to talk to my teenagers about what safe, loving, caring, gentle, consenting sex looks like versus the orgies or whips and chains they may be seeing on the Internet. Yes, they walked away from me mid-sentence. This is one life lesson I could not physically 'show' my kids, like how to tie their shoelaces or to open up a savings account in a bank.

We talk about how the world has become sexually open with trans and gay, and how wonderful this is and at the same time, so confusing and so hard. No hiding, just being accepted as you, with multiple generations trying to understand. We share thoughts about how your sexual preference really is no one's business, knowing that is easy for us to say, as we are mainly in traditional heterosexual relationships.

As we hit middle age, we talk about the reality of sex drives diminishing. Say what? Yup. We talk about how awful that would be, and the reasons why and how to fix that up, rocket-speed. We pile each other with a mountain load of sex resources, websites, podcasts, teachings, tools and strategies. I recently did a check in with the younger female generation, and yup, they also do a lot of sex talking and sharing.

Doesn't this all sound healthy? Well, I absolutely think so, until I talk to the boys and see where they are at in all this sex talk. And I got *nada*.

I can't understand why men are not talking about sex, when typically, men can be deemed friskier than women. And I know a few women who are going to challenge me on that statement! I would think guys would want to do some sharing on one of their favourite topics. Who could not benefit from talking through and learning some new moves from their buddies? Or sharing a mind-blowing sexual experience? I certainly hear men talk about their mind-blowing golf game score or mind-blowing big engine on their new car.

This girl sex talk versus boy sex talk became a revelation to me one summer. My husband and I rented a charming oceanfront summer home where we hosted our friends and family each week. We had a

Mind DOODLES

revolving door of people coming and going. Every night was a party, and it was freaking fabulous. One week my husband had just his guy friends over. As I was popping in and out of the patio conversations with the guys, I realized how different my conversations had been on the same patio with my girlfriends just nights before.

The boys were on and on with loads of sports talk—yeah, I know, another surprise. Lots of back-in-the-day memory talk, lots of teasing each other talk, lots of weird trivia or crossword games and even scientific talk about gravity and ocean. This is where I yawned and went to bed. But before I tuned out the scientific jargon, I was curious. I asked them if they ever talked about sex?

The guys didn't skip a beat and said Nope. No sex talk. *Nada*.

When I asked why, they said their mom and dad never openly talked about sex. Or they were raised to keep quiet on the topic. What? So were all my middle-aged girlfriends, and that clearly didn't stop us!

I say, boys, bust the sex conversation wide open. Go for it! Seriously, why are you ripping yourself off? Not only to learn from your friends for yourself, but to role model to the next generation that it's healthy to openly talk about sex. And it's fun. I asked my husband to help me wrap up this topic with some words of male sex-talk inspiration, and guess what? I got *nada*.

THE "C" WORD

I don't even know where to begin this one. I just know that I have to try, even though it will likely come out as a big jumble of blah.

So, in life, the way I see it, some of us are charmed, and by some fluke we meet our life partner at a young age. By some miracle we grow up together without growing substantially apart and keep the foundation of love. I know the fluke and miracle part can remain in question.

I made that all sound really simple, especially as I look at my fifty-something-year-old husband of thirty something years, eating an electric-blue freezie in his cargo shorts and his Marvel Comic T-shirt while listening to 1970s/80s rock that he refuses to expand from since he was a teenager. Note, I am grateful the tube socks are long gone. Where do I go from here?

Some people meet the love of their life later in their years. Some people spend a lot of energy planning and meeting their partner and some partnerships are unexpected. Some people get love second-or-third-time lucky. And some people get absolutely ripped off and lose their love early, and for the blessed ones, later. Or some people just don't find the love of their life at all. Then some people think they are in the love of their life relationship, years even, to discover they in fact aren't. Perhaps never been all along, imploding their entire relationship and life. That is an entirely different topic, for another book, by another writer.

Mind DOODLES

    Falling in love and staying in love are quite different. You get at least a three-year falling-in-love honeymoon period, maybe even up to five years. Then, in not so obvious ways, the Love-Effort starts to kick in. Effort to like or put up with each other's friends or families. Effort to compromise when making decisions together on buying furniture. Effort to decide where to go on your vacation. Yes, even effort to have the energy to have sex. Then the effort escalates into responsibility. Mortgage, earning enough income, a dog, dentist appointments, saving money, careers, house cleaning, car repairs, kids, managing mental health, physical health, caring for elderly family members—the responsibility list goes on and on.

    In all this effort, you know you have Love-Hope if you can still make each other laugh. Or if you still stop for that oh-so-safe, warm hug in the middle of the grocery store. Or if you still catch a glimpse of your partner in the morning getting ready for work and feel admiration. Or if you can still find things to do together that give you your fun injection. Or if you can still feel proud of even the smallest acts, like putting together an Ikea desk with the instructions in Swedish. And the biggest Love-Hope—being able to talk things through.

    Yes, the "C Word." I said it. The Allstar C Word…Communication.

    Now, I know for many, seeking the partner that can have those daily deep reflective conversations is a top priority. And for the other many, it may just mean talking through and understanding situations as they pop up without throwing some object at their head, or while you throw a hissy fit to get their attention. Whatever meaningful communication you both need just make it happen. If you don't know or can't, all I know is that it could possibly sink you. Yes, the tough part will be to really know what type of communication each of you need and respecting that style. Warning: it may be very painful.

    Also know your partner most likely will not be able to give you ALL the communication you need. Really, think about how can one person truly give you all of it? So, dig into the C Word and figure that out pronto. Like what the late great Gordie from Tragically Hip sang about—being together constantly because that's what we figured married people did. If you need emotional communication, and your partner is empty in the tank, you are going to have to put a Plan B into action and seek that conversation from your friends or family.

And along the way in all this C Word effort, you both just keep trying, trying and trying—without giving up. Giving up can go in so many dangerous directions. Drifting apart, lying, cheating, reduced intimacy, unhappiness, resentment, and bitterness. On top of all this talking, and heroic C Word effort, you have to also be on top of your game with the ongoing changes. We age, we change, we have experiences, we change, circumstances change, we change, we learn, and we change. So, what worked last year in communication may need something new this year, or what wasn't an effort five years ago, has become a must-have. Also know, the C Word may seem extra hard at times, even when it shouldn't. The fun never stops.

I'm not saying I have any secret sauce for my marriage, and in fact, we definitely are more of a wing-it type couple. I think fluke and miracle could be used to describe our relationship, with a "meant to be" thrown in there. The C Word has always been present, but often with great effort.

Recently my husband retired from his long-time career as a banker of thirty-seven years. The retirement was over-the-top well deserved and I agreed to work forever to keep our income humming along. Life as we knew it, changed. I went to work, and my husband didn't. I know that doesn't seem off the charts, but living with each other for thirty years, and suddenly not getting up at the same time together each day to go to work and come home at night, was a change.

With both of us in active careers, the weekends were always treasured. My husband liked to relax on the weekends, and well, if you

Mind DOODLES

are making it through this book you know I like to play. My husband would welcome the quiet and be more than happy to stay home while I ventured off to go dancing or hiking. This worked for thirty years, until the retirement change. I stayed on course for the dancing and hiking weekends, while my husband realized he didn't need to relax on the weekends anymore as he was relaxed all the time in retirement.

Yes, we had to use the C Word to figure out this change.

Even after being together all that time, the conversation was a little awkward and uncomfortable. I don't recall any swear words being thrown around, but maybe I didn't hear them. Anyways, the point is we had to C Word whether we wanted to or not, to move forward. And we have. I think. Just kidding, yes, we have!

Phew! Are you tired yet? Hang in there, I got two more things to say.

Every partnership is unique. What works in C Word world for your best friends, your neighbours, your parents, may not work for you. But I think what you can do is take the best of the best of all the healthy partnerships you are honoured to witness, and then go for it. Also know, what you see on the surface is probably not what is truly happening behind the scenes. So, seek those relationships that come in the rare form of transparency and honesty. Learn all you can.

My last words of reflection, which is based on my personal bias only, is communicating your partnership values and sticking to them. Make them foolproof, uncrackable and keep those babies strong!

If you met my husband and I at a party for the first time without any background on us, you would be thinking one of two things: Huh? What the? These two are actually married? Or, I can't see these two lasting very long! Let's take some bets.

You see, we are opposites. Opposites in our views, opinions, personalities and emotions. But what we aren't opposite in, is our commitment to communication and our relationship values. Strong work ethic, trust, respect and honesty. I know these values are a bit boring, but they are real. These values have carried us through some dark times, and carried us higher in the higher times, without ever being compromised.

Consider yourself lucky if your paths are crossed by pure intervention and you find the love of your life. Get your values in alignment, know you've got to high-gear your efforts on all fronts, and keep the C Word alive.

You got this.

Losing YOUR BIGGEST FANS

I wish I didn't know about this yet, but I do.

When I was thirty years old, I was accused of being a "silver spoon" kid. Yeah, what the heck does that mean? Well, it means being born into a privileged life and perhaps protected from trauma.

I absolutely was privileged, but not in the money sense, in the parent sense. My mom took on the role of the traditional 1950s housewife—and still proud to her last day! Dad selflessly took on two jobs to make that happen. They both were at as many of my ball games in their rickety green and white striped lawn chairs as I could remember. We lived in a neighbourhood where the neighbours were like family, sharing garlic and ripe red tomatoes over the fence. This was where our family home stood strong for over forty years.

I always had a new school outfit every September from the Sears catalogue—and trust me, that was the end-of-summer highlight. I ate like a queen from our fresh vegetable garden in the backyard with homemade soup such as borscht. I can still see my kids on the back deck with their grandparents, shelling the peas for the soup in the warm sun. I was role-modelled a loving marriage where my parents held hands every night going to sleep. We played Monopoly on Sunday nights as a family where I got to be the car. Mom taught me how to make the best homemade perogies that dripped in bacon bits and cabbage rolls that melted in your mouth. I enjoyed fishing trips with Dad, finding remote lakes down old dusty logging roads, and I fondly remember our family wienie roasts by the river, complete with cream sodas and stick whittling.

Of course, it wasn't all sunshine, unicorns and rainbows. My parents had high expectations, and their own demands on my brother and me. They had strong views on how life should be lived. But bottom line: I had the highest privilege of having two unconditional people in my life that I could count on, trust with my entire being and lean into every single day, the good along with the bad. They were my biggest fans.

I had a complete safety net and a fall-back position I could always rely on. I always had a home base that never changed. This home base was so solid that I still had my same bedroom, with the same rust-brown shag carpet, with the same bed I slept in growing up. My brother also had his own bed and bedroom, except my brother had a retro blue flower carpet that I didn't even notice until I hit my 40s. Every time I went home to visit and dropped my sleepover stuff in my old bedroom, I was still expecting my Shaun Cassidy and John Stamos posters to be up. Where did those precious posters of those hunks with their feathered hair go, anyways?

Not only did this home base stay solid, but my parents did too. Whenever I came home, I had the luxury of still having all my favourite meals made by Mom. She was even happy to do my laundry and hang it on the clothesline, so it was nice and fresh. I know, spoiled. For the longest time, we still had the same banana-yellow finger-dialling rotary telephone on the wall, with the long cord that wrapped around to the kitchen. My parents were technology-amazed the day we bought them their first cordless phone. The neighbours also stayed the same, greeting me over the fence with a warm hello and chit chat, giving me an update on their grownup kids who I used to babysit. Every home visit, Dad would tour me around the yard, showing off his latest juicy-apple-creations from the tree, or the crops of plums that were about to ripen.

If this is called being a "silver spoon" kid, then I am honoured, and you can stick that label right on my forehead. I know not every kid gets this privilege, and not every kid gets their own two personal fans.

Speaking only from this perspective, how do you prepare yourself for losing your biggest fans? It will happen, and it does. And it sure did to me. We know for sure that we are born and then we will die.

However, we spend a lot of time in the Birth Preparation Arena of being born, with naming ceremonies, colourful balloons, religious baptisms, announcements, baby showers, adorable gifts and over-the-top kid bedroom decorating. Some of us spend none to some time in the Death Preparation Arena. Then there is the preparation on losing your biggest fans, that seems to be lost. Whether it is a family member or close friend or a life partner—I know you have a biggest fan somewhere in that mix.

Our biggest fans allow us to take chances, to take risks in life. Knowing they will catch us as we fall—or at least pick us up, take us to get that broken bone looked at, and find us a shot of whiskey. They help us get out of sticky situations. We can count on them for always being on the other end of the phone when we need that voice.

Our biggest fans make us feel like we are invincible. They give us confidence and courage to apply for that seemingly out-of-reach career job. That we can do anything we set our minds to. They help us believe that anything is possible. And when things are impossible, that failure is a good thing—life lessons for the next thing, or not meant to be.

Our biggest fans coach and teach us. They give us practical tools on how to budget or pay your taxes. They show us how to grocery shop and meal plan for the week. Or how to do a stellar resume and winning cover letter. They coach us on handling intimate relationships, in strengthening friendships, or when it is time to let go. They inspire us in making healthy choices. They teach us how to parent, how to cope, how to handle stress, how to look for the "signs."

Mind DOODLES

Our biggest fans help us be resourceful, connect us and find opportunities. They support us on helping us find what path to take or learn when to turn around and go back. They help us get through school, choose our life directions, challenge us to look at religion and be open to all spiritualities. Our biggest fans direct us in looking at all perspectives and angles.

Our biggest fans nurture our spirit. They know what lifts us up and what can bring us down. Our biggest fans give us encouragement. They encourage us to try new things. They tell us to learn a new skill, play an instrument, join a sports team, climb a mountain, see different countries and embrace cultures and lifestyles.

Our biggest fans understand us, they have lived our history. They speak the truth, even if it's hard to hear. And sometimes they don't speak at all, knowing we just need silence and physical presence. Our biggest fans give us strength. With mental health, with physical health. Our biggest fans let us be who we truly are. Let the guard right down. Show true vulnerability. Express our hurt—when all we want to do is shut the world away and know that we can't.

How do we prepare ourselves for when our biggest fans, well, just physically vanish from life?

Start paying attention, like right now. I know that is going to be hard. It feels very natural to take our biggest fans for granted. But stop. We may not agree with all the coaching, nurturing, direction that we receive from our biggest fans, but start wading through and taking the "best of the best." Or take time to listen and absorb and save the information in our memory bank to be checked out later in life when we need it. If our memory is short, start writing it down. If we have a good memory, take more time reflecting to have it really stick.

Ask questions, understand our biggest fans' journey, do a video, go through old photo albums and write on the back of the pictures, do a voice recording—gather the information that is meaningful. One of my favourite moments was listening and recording the life stories of my grandma, Gee Gee. She talked for hours about the old school general store they owned and what life was like in the 1900s. I also loved the time I spent doing a road trip with Dad, then mom going down memory lane on their family farms. I grabbed our five-pound video recorder and decided to track this history. I taped dad showing me his first tree he planted as a young boy, then Mom showing me her first home, where mud was used to bond the logs together so her house could stay standing. I even dragged that heavy recorder out with my uncle, hopping farm fences, to record the birth of calves in the middle of the night—yes, I am feeling scarred by that visual.

All our biggest fans want is for us to live our best life. And if they have helped us do that, tell them. That is the legacy we all live for at the end of any day.

Why don't we also honour them while they are alive and kicking? I know there is the traditional birthday or annual celebrations, but why not bring it up a notch?

One of my best life memories was hosting a "Pot Party" in my mom's honour—and I'm not talking about pots and pans type pot. For those of you that knew my mom, she was one classy, practical and straight-laced woman who we fondly called Baba. When my dad, who we fondly called Dido, passed away a few years ago, Baba was completely lost. Her health declined and she spent a lot of time away from her small-town family home and started spending time in the big city suburbs with me and my family in our home.

Over a few years, Baba met our fun and crazy pals. She met our spirited neighbours who we share a few rums with on the back deck versus the over-the-fence tomato sharing Baba was used to. Baba was curious about all the new people and lifestyles she was meeting and asked a lot of questions. One day, she asked me if she could try smoking pot. I was shocked—and trust me, that does not happen

Mind DOODLES

often. Sweet little square Baba smoking weed? I tried to imagine it and just couldn't.

At the time of Baba's stoner request, her health was getting worse and her end of life was possibly around the corner. I called all the doctors and asked the nurses if the "devil's weed" adventure was going to kill her on the spot, and they laughed, and everyone said go for it. So, I did. And Treena-like, why not turn this into a Pot Party?

So, in honour of Baba, I invited our closest friends and neighbours to this unique event with a promise of lots of munchies. My teenage kids thought this was awesome, that their grandma was going to be puffing on some dope. In fact, I asked them to source the goods. They thought that was great. I questioned myself, as their mother, if I was being a horrible role model, and I decided I was being a great role model. I was showing my kids about honour. Oh yeah, you can spin anything to be favourable.

It was interesting to me to discover the mixture of reactions from each guest I invited to the Pot Party. Some of the guests who had not smoked pot before thought this was a great opportunity to try it. Heck yeah! My husband and a handful of our closest friends did not want to have anything to do with these shenanigans—as they felt this was not a good idea for sweet little Baba. Some of the guests said they would come to be part of the honour but not smoke the ganja, and some said they were "unsure" and would wait to feel the vibe. Some guests said it was about time we had a Pot Party. One of my best friends explained that it's common in many cultures to honour death wishes, by forming a circle.

You got it, the Pot Party just turned Pot Circle.

The guests arrived, took their seat in the "Pot Circle" and my teenage kids presented a gift to their Baba—the guest of honour. Yes, the gift was thoughtful and took the party to a new level. Baba was outfitted in her very own green pot leaf snapback hat, a Bob Marley metallic

T-shirt, and bling necklace complete with a diamond spinning marijuana leaf. Sweet little Baba looked the part of a drug-dealing gangster. We were ready. As the joint was lit, my friend spoke about the "Pot Circle" honour and traditional meaning. As we passed the grass, we all took a turn saying our caring words to Baba and my heart could not have been fuller of love for my people, as I watched Mom enjoy every word and every toke.

You can imagine the rest of the party was full of giggles and a large consumption of good food, complete with Baba's favourites. Yup, we had the smell of Baba's pork bellies being fried throughout the house, wafting in blend with the hemp. A lovely smelling combo. As one of Baba's closest friends slid around in her slippery socks on my hardwood floor, thinking she was on roller skates, I knew this was the best Pot Party, ever, celebrating Baba's wish.

And for goodness sake, do not have any regrets. Say what you need to say, do what you need to do with your biggest fans! Make it a regular occurrence. You can never have too many memories or have too many words of inspiration from your biggest fans. And if you can't say what you need to say, come to terms with it now, and move on, guilt free.

On the emotional front, do get ready for the tsunami of heartbreak. It will be pain like no other, and that you will have to accept. Cry through it, rage through it, feel through it—as your loss will be large, no matter what age you lose your biggest fan. I personally think time may not heal, but rather, just gives you some really deep grief scars. I think all we can do is just accept the loss when our hearts and head are ready to do so and know we will continually feel the heartache. Sometimes dull and sometimes full on knife-through-your-heart kind.

If we are lucky to outlive our biggest fans, we will all have to deal with this. If we have prepared and accepted it in our own way, and when the grief doesn't knock us off our feet each day, we will know

Mind DOODLES

we have honoured our biggest fan legacy and that is the best anyone can do.

Our biggest fans are our biggest gift. But this gift does have an expiry date.

Bucket List
WRITE THEN STRIKE THAT SHIT OFF

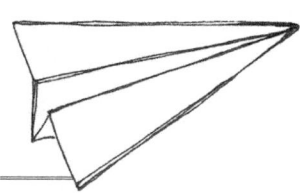

Wikipedia defines a Bucket List as a list of activities someone wants to do before they die, because it's things they want to do before they "kick the bucket." A slang term meaning, "to die."

Okay, now that we got that spelled out, do you have a pen and a piece of paper? Do you own a computer with an Excel spreadsheet? Do you have a calendar app? Most likely there is already a Bucket List app! Do you have a phone that can record your voice? If you have said yes to any of the above questions you can have your very own Bucket List. Seriously true.

If I am sounding frustrated, I think that I actually am.

So many people walk around talking about what they could do or what they should do and what they want to do. They also talk about what is in their way of doing and what they aren't doing. They also say what they want to do "one day," what they don't have time to do, and on and on.

Come on, just freaking do it.

Recording something permanently for you to look at, is the best start to keeping yourself accountable. This is the best hope of scratching something off your "list." Which, by the way, feels really, really satisfying when you see that line or tick mark beside your bucket item as completed and the photo shutter of memories fly by in your mind.

Mind DOODLES

I love doing this.

The next step is to give yourself a due date—remember, this is why I am writing this book, tick tock. And keep it easy, maybe knock off one thing a year. Think about it. One thing out of 365 days. One thing out of twelve months. One thing annually.

And your bucket list doesn't even have to be filled with jumping out of planes or riding an elephant. It can be volunteering with seniors once a month at their happy hour, taking a Thai cooking class for one evening; getting a tattoo; and it can be reading this book from cover to cover. Your bucket list can really be anything you want to achieve that would bring you great reward.

For me, the learned lesson on writing then striking off the bucket list items, is simply to not even consider any excuses. I don't allow any self doubt to creep into my mind. I just put my head down, write it on the list and then go for it. I don't check in with anyone if they think it's a good idea. I pick things only I want to do, which means, my selection committee always gets my majority vote. Sometimes I invite people and sometimes I don't. Some bucket list items are for me only, and that is part of the experience, part of the bucket list prize.

I believe bucket list items can be for all sorts of reasons. It can be for your typical personal growth reasons, like becoming more confident or less serious. It can simply be for fun. It can be about looking forward to having something to daydream about when you are looking out the window. It can be about discovery. For me, it's about the challenge. I love throwing bucket list items on the list that are a bit hard to reach or have a bit of a risky flavour. Hmmm—I wonder what a risky flavour would taste like? Spicy cinnamon with a dash of tangy orange?

As I age, the bucket list items seem to be getting bolder and bolder. Maybe it's because my kids are now young adults and can strongly live life on their own. Or maybe it's because after fifty, there is a fast track to sixty, seventy then eighty? Even writing that was lightning-bolt fast.

Dusting off my memory, my earliest bucket list item was when I was a teenager. Growing up in a small town, I had the strongest urge to flee and explore. I was an avid reader and I read books about city lights, grand opportunities and an entire world of possibility. My first bucket list item was to live in the city. At eighteen, I found myself in downtown Vancouver, twirling with my beret in the middle of the busy street of Robson, just like Mary Tyler Moore—yes, Google her. I was in City Love. TICK.

Next was a good-old-fashioned backpack trip to Europe. Growing up, travelling wasn't part of the culture in our family or with my friends. So, once I arrived in the city, meeting people my age, I was learning all about the wonders of travel. Ten countries in thirty days with my trusty backpack. I was in Travel Love. TICK.

I think it can also get fuzzy between life goals and bucket list items. For me, came a career, marriage, kids, and a house with a white picket fence. But the fence was brown. For the purpose of this topic, let's coin these as life goals. So, getting back to the bucket list, there were many items popping up here and there. From singing lessons to taking swimming lessons for my first triathlon attempt (which was an auto-backwards-tick due to no-can-do, as I need water wings to float, which I still think counts as a half of a tick for effort.) There was also powerlifting feats, tennis tournaments, cycling Napa Valley, becoming a certified fitness instructor (oh yeah, boot camp, baby) and Costa Rica yoga retreats in the jungle—the list and the striking was actively on fire.

I also had a bit of a bucket list cliché streak going. Got the good 'ol first tattoo at thirty. Then for the Big-Ticket bucket list item: getting my motorcycle license and buying myself a hot, sexy Harley.

I picked forty to get my Harley, as I knew I should be a responsible enough rider by then, knowing I had a family to think about in case I went all Evel Knievel—sigh, once again, Google it. Plus, it took me all those years to save some extra 'toy' cash. I still re-

Mind DOODLES

member the day my friend Tom and I went to go get my bike. Tom was born riding, and I trusted him completely to ride my Harley-baby home. I was so freaking excited, like a kid on Christmas morning with all those Santa presents ready to rip open. I also remember how hungover my friend Tom was as we were driving to get my new bike and having to pull over every twenty minutes. I worked hard at shrugging off questioning myself if he was the right guy to ride my new shiny toy home. Tom made it home no problem—what a guy. My first ride was euphoric, with the wind blowing through my hair, my new black Harley leather jacket making me feel extra cool, and the pure feeling of freedom. I was Harley-baby in Love. TICK.

Ahhhh, now how do you follow that bucket-list act? Well, I managed okay, with a cooking school in Tuscany; three more backpacking trips hiking through remote backcountry mountains; a cycle trip through New Zealand; spending time with a monk in Japan. I am now tracking a bucket list of adventuring three new countries a year and have lost count of the total. And of course, I am smack-in-the-middle of a bucket list implementation, which is writing this quirky, entertaining book. Half TICK.

So, what's on the list ahead, you ask? I know I want to head in a musical direction—who knows, maybe I have hidden talents and I will be on the next *Some Canadian Babe Got Talent* show. At some point I want to volunteer my business skills in a faraway country and live there for a year or do an impactful mission of sorts. I think a fourth career could be in the future with a bucket list TICK and am toying with a culinary school. Then thinking about a fifth career in starting my own Canadian adventure business called Off the Beaten Path.

I'm not sure what happened with my Barbara Walters (geez, another Google, I bet), journalist bucket list item or Oprah takeover. I better put that back on the list. Also dreaming about living in different places around Canada a few months at a time to explore our culture across the provinces. Montreal would be a cool city to live in and checking out Newfoundland. I also have a TED Talk written down—perhaps about this book. Maybe on bucket lists? Really, who knows. I just keep writing that shit down and striking it off. What I can tell you is that the list is growing faster than I can strike off. So many places to explore, mind blowing things to do, and yup, I am fifty. Remember the sixty to eighty zoom?

Bottom line: life is short. Do stuff you want to do. We can get stuck in routine. We can get stuck in making other people happy. We can get stuck in the "I don't have enough time" syndrome. And we can just plain get stuck. But really, we don't have to. I know I made this sound easy. But it truly is.

If you are stuck, you are the only person in your own way. So get out of your way and write, then strike that shit off.

GO Play

As your world turns with unexpected pressures, and disappointment and the creeping feeling of overwhelm knocks on your life door—I have two screaming words: GO PLAY.

Play can be whatever you need it to be. Play a team sport. Play in the snow. Play a prank. Play with your dog Spot by the river. Play with your friends on a night downtown. Play on a road trip without a map and get lost. Play Nicky Nicky Nine Doors. Play a card trick. Play squash. Play on a hop-on-and-off bus in a city. Play the bongo drums. Play the game of Popcorn on a Trampoline (sorry, Auntie Merion, for popping you too hard). Play poker with your pals—clothing optional. Play in unknown territory with your kayak. Perform in a play. Play music bingo. Play Barbies or Legos with a little kid. Play pinball.

Just. Go. Play.

I used to take this bootcamp class where every Friday was "zoo play," which meant we did exercises we used to do as a kid. We did the good 'ol crab crawl race, we played tag, we raced like monkeys on all fours and we laughed like crazy while doing it. And boy, did we sweat.

When I first started dating my husband, we would pack up whatever we could get our hands on and head to White Rock beach to go play. Before all the new buildings and restaurants, there used to be huge fields of grass on the edge of the beach. We would find our spot,

Mind DOODLES

open the bag of whatever we could get our hands on, and go play. We played football. We put our baseball gloves on and played catch. We dug out the badminton rackets and played. And my favourite, was running around and playing with the kite. That beach always had the best wind and that play day made me happy.

Easygoing play just makes everything seem better and somehow lighter. The pressure of yesterday, no longer seems that big a deal. You start to question why you were so disappointed and decide to not be. And boom, you think, overwhelmed? Who? No way, not me.

Weirdly enough, some of the best play I have seen are with my husband's pals. When they get together, they really do play, and it can be for hours. Beers in hand, they play informal sports trivia, challenging each other with old hockey or ball stats along with all the new stats. They have a kooky game of Seinfeld Trivia, testing each other on where is this line and what Seinfeld episode is it from. They have all the old school movies lined up in their minds like *Caddyshack* or *Slap Shot*, and quiz each other on scenes and characters. I have seen them play crosswords together in the sunshine with their shirts off, sun tanning and still using number four Hawaiian Tropic oil!

I have been in awe watching them play a game of catch where they add game twists such as making your left shoulder the target for five points. I just realized; I have never really heard them have a lengthy, intense conversation. I think their playing is their conversation—something to ponder.

My point is, whatever play means to you, make the time and do it. And don't count playing video games or Candy Crush on your iPhone as your play. That is a cheat.

Figure out your play.

Playing gives you that life break. Resets your worrying brain. And the big reward is recharging your batteries for the days ahead. If you make room in your life to play, you will make better decisions as your head will be clear. The heavy burden of life stuff won't feel so heavy. You will have re-found energy to tackle down the tough stuff.

I have so much play in my life, I don't even know how to explain it. Maybe I have too much and am in overload? Nah. Flipping through your photos is always fun, as they are full of play. I am loving the pics of where my niece and nephew took us out in the bush with their rifles and we played shooting at the pumpkin and pop cans. Fun gun play!

I have thousands, yes really, thousands of pictures of my friends and I playing. Top plays would be with our "little men," okay, well, my "little men," dressed as firemen or lifeguards or whatever career of choice. They hang on the edge of your martini glass or a wine bottle—they are playful and fun. We have had them dancing on straws (aka a pole) taking some cheeky playful videos. We even used them as barrettes in my friend's big curly hair one night. Holy playing, Batman.

My friends and I have seen many "playful gifts" such as hot pink decorative bras complete with fuzzy birds or blinged-out visors. We have fun with a big blow-up doll named Billy Joel that we dress up and take out for a good body surf on the dance floor. We also have fun with our mini blow-up doll named Billy Joel Jr who we have taken kayaking and on many road trips, hanging out on the dash of the car. We have played with fake mustaches when out for fancy cocktails in Yaletown. We have played dress-up at the Fairmont Hotel for High Tea.

We have played in swimming pools with confetti-filled toys. We have played insane drunk characters called Ab, Fab and Bubbles with playful English accents at Halloween parties. We have worn matching crazy outfits more times than I can count, at concerts and just because. We have played at many dance parties, on yachts, on hotel suite couches and always, always, in my living room. We have played Jell-O-shot throwing contests adding splashes of orange and red accent goop to my walls. We have played on the dance floor at nightclubs and bars, playing tag and peek-a-boo around the bopping crowd.

Mind DOODLES

Of course, I have seen my kids play. And geez, did they play. From kid toys to young teenage boys playing big-pointy-stick tag out in the bush. Yes, I put an end to that one, as I was sure someone was going to lose an eye. I have seen the aftermath of play during the sticky-marshmallow fights that could not be removed from the TV screen.

I loved our annual family snowball fight that always got ugly and ended badly with tears—by the boys I might add. Plus, the endless games of basketball, playing Twenty-One in our driveway. I loved the road hockey games playing goalie and getting pucks at the head. Lots of ice hockey play on the frozen lake in the winter, where I know my brother-in-law cross-checked me from behind and I landed hard on my ass. That one is no fun play. Play then moved to countless games of Beer Pong in our dining room, on our patio, on our lawn and even in our hallway. Then there was the outdoor play, with crazy cliffside hikes or kayaking to our summer house rental on our own private island. There was also lots of traditional play with board games. Loads of play with full-on card games of Canasta and Wizard. Play, play and more play.

I am sure there are tests done on your endorphins or some other scientific fact, that even looking forward to play or reflecting on your play, will give you new zest for life. I always liked Saturday as my play day. After a busy week, knowing I can coast into the weekend with some play, makes everything alright.

Now, GO PLAY!

THE FRIENDSHIP
Web

Don't think this is going to be a no-brainer topic that you can skim over. You don't want to mess this one up and speed read through. If anything, you want to get out your drink with the little umbrella, sit back and really pay attention. No matter what age you are, the simplest of friendships can get, well, a little sticky, messy, web-like.

One of my friends says her mom taught her you should be able to count your best friends on one hand. Being more than halfway through my life now, I must conclude her mom was absolutely right. Not only are there best friends, but now so many different types of friends. Sometimes I think I need a tracking system to keep it all straight.

Starting with Best Friends—these are your wing men or women. Ones you can count on for anything. Ones that won't judge. Ones you can trust with your life. Ones you can't wait to see. Ones you tell all with. Ones you want to share experiences with. Ones you share the good, the bad and the ugly with. Ones you can simply cry with or just belly laugh your way through a weekend without any deep conversations. Your vulnerability crew. Your lifers. The ones that won't let you down and totally get you. They are your people; they are your tribe.

Then there are your Close Friends. Not quite a Bestie, as maybe they don't always come through with time or availability, for what you need in a friendship connection. But you love them unconditionally anyways. They are good people, in fact, the best. You keep these close friends close to your heart and always give them a second chance to show up—which they do, eventually. These close friends are worth your perseverance.

Then there are the History Friends. Ones you may have grownup with or went to high school, college or uni with. Or maybe you met at a job or travelling and had some sort of Aha! deep-connecting time or experience. It is a bond that can't be broken, and they will always be a friend fan favourite.

Then there are your Acquaintance Friends. These are your casual buddies. You hang with them when only a certain crew gets together. Or you may spend time with them on specific things that you have in common, like hitting a wine tasting on your favourite blends, or shared interest in heavy metal music to hit concerts with. Or maybe you have volunteered together at fundraising events. They add spark to your life journey. But they also come and go. I am guessing they may be a majority of your social media pals. Or a majority of your work mates. Maybe even a majority of your community life connections.

Then there is your Party Gang. People you celebrate life with. You may only see them on special occasions or for vacays. Or maybe you can only relate to them on the dance floor. They are your fun factors and the must-haves during big-deal gigs. They bring the fireworks at midnight. They elevate your life high, higher.

Whatever friend arena your friends land in, they all add value to your life. And if they don't, I got two words: ditch 'em. Let's circle back to that later.

Know that within those varied friendship types there are many ebbs and flows. Within all those ebbs and flows can come an endless list of confusion. You got it, here comes the sticky web. A friend that was part of your Party Gang, may stop showing up. There may not be any explanation or even any response and they may ghost you—boo. They leave you feeling, WTF?

A Close Friend may want to move into your Bestie circle. However, you may have decided you are not taking any further Best Friend requests. By the way, there was a great *Seinfeld* episode where Jerry announced he was not taking any further friend applications—brilliant! Or maybe you just aren't feeling the Close Friend to Best Friend moving vibe.

Here's something: an Acquaintance Friend may not even consider you a friend—yet another WTF? A History Friend may decide to ditch you last minute on an invite, as maybe they are not feeling as past-connected to you as you thought. How do we get this friendship stuff all right and not wrong? I have to tell you, I don't have any of this figured out. Nope, not even close.

But what I can tell you is to expect it, be open to it and be ready to ride some of those friendship waves. I have learned that in friendships, the relationship expectations can really go off the charts and in different directions. Sounds like a marriage, doesn't it?

Once I had this friendship that was on the border of Close Friend to Best Friend. We had a regular hangout date each week, plus we often got together on weekends with a group of friends. We had the very best times laughing—as she was over-the-top hilarious. At the time of our friendship, I was on a very intimate journey with my family. I shared this private time with her, every step of the way. She was a great listener and provided a strong shoulder to lean into. I felt very close to her and assumed she felt the same. Then out of nowhere, our regular hangout dates started to get rescheduled by my Close-to-Best-friend friend—stay with me. Our weekend group nights out also started to evaporate. I was missing my friend.

As I like to tackle confusion head on, I straight-up asked what was happening to our friendship. I got the 'ol "everything is fine" response.

Mind DOODLES

I tried again and received the same "everything is fine." But I knew it wasn't, and without any conversation to understand what was going on, I couldn't do anything about it. I had to accept, move on and then, boom—our friendship ended. I still miss this friendship and wonder from time to time if she does too.

I reflect that maybe when you age, and you start to come to grips with your friendships, you let yourself get closer to your friends. I also reflect that when you age, the exact opposite could happen, and you could pull back from getting too close in your friendships. It also may have nothing to do with age and could be all about your baggage and recent relationship experiences. See? I really have no idea.

All I know is to expect your friendships to sometimes be at different levels, and when you hit the bonanza, there is no better feeling to be at the same level. Ebb and flow, I say, ebb and flow. For me, I know I can bring a lot of fierce love to my best friendships. I am like the Italians: I love deeply, strongly and forever. I take my Best Friend status seriously, and one of my favourite things on this planet is being a best friend and having best friends. You definitely want me as your maid of honour if you want a kick-ass shower, stag and wedding speech.

However, not everyone is like the Italians, loving and best-friending so fiercely. This can cause some of that sticky-web-mess I was talking about. Friend management. Who knew? Now you know, if you haven't already figured it out long ago.

Circling back to the "ditch 'em" commentary, your friendships will ultimately bring some drama and time-consuming factors into the relationship at some point. If they bring great value to you, and life has just given you some friendship sticky-webs to unstick, then figure it out. If the friendship is sucking you dry of energy and time you will never get back, then never fear the friendship break-up. All the same relationship rules apply—be respectful, communicate the reasons, be honest and say so long in the nicest way.

The friendship break-up will be hard, it will be emotional, and a little heart-achy. Don't be a coward. As gently as possible let this friend know why you are breaking up with them. It is the right thing to do.

The last thing I have to say about friends is, make time for them. Depending on what age you are reading this, there are many life things coming your way where you may want to low-prioritize your friendship time. It could be when you find that significant romantic relationship and find yourself not having so much time for your friends. It could be when you hit that ever-growing mountain of responsibility zone with career and kids—finding yourself with little friend energy left at the end of the day. It could be that you are going through a rough time, where all you want to do is push your friends away.

There are temptations everywhere to have your friendships be the first relationship to let go versus valuing those friends with all you got. Friends give you interesting perspectives on life. They give you much needed life breaks. They give you some of the best laughs ever. They give you playful memories. They give your heart emotional support. They can challenge you to see things differently or validate your current vision. They can make you feel oh-so-good about yourself. They can make you feel smart. They can make you feel young. They can give you a helping hand when you need it and even when you don't. They can be right by your side during sad times and right by your side during happy times.

Friendship web or not, friendships are worth all that potential sticky mess.

Mind DOODLES

GET OUTSIDE YOUR Bubble

We all live in a bubble. Our bubble consists of our day-to-day routine of responsibility. Our current living style, our past and our environment. We may be in our bubble making ourselves better, or perhaps not caring. We may be life-surviving or maybe we are striving for change. We may be balanced in our bubble or we may be bobbing around. Our bubble has our family, relationships, acquaintances, neighbours and colleagues all tucked inside. Our bubble could be a mix of social, health, wellness, charity and career, that are part of our life. In the bubble we could be dealing with what's in front of us today, or it could be fighting demons from the past. We may be trying to get ready for our future.

Each day may blend into the next, or maybe you hold on to each day. You may also be holding tightly to the past. As time ticks, we can only bring into our day and lives what we know from our experiences and where we have engaged. We life-react based on our life knowledge, which all lives in our bubble.

The way we treat people, our ethics, our personalities, our judgement—is based on what we know in the bubble. If we keep our world small inside our bubble, those will be the only tools, knowledge and tricks that we may reach out to or draw upon.

Where the "H E double-hockey-sticks" am I going with all this bubble talk, you may ask?

I can totally hear you: "enough of the bubble already!" It's time to encourage you to get outside your bubble. I am talking about travel. I am talking about getting outside your hood and having new experiences. I know not everyone is down for travelling. Not everyone is comfortable leaving their home court, their safe comfy space. Not everyone is up for meeting new people. But if I am able to plant the seed, then my job here is done.

Yup, I'm going to go for the Big Guns right off the hop and head right into travelling. I'm not sure what has happened to me over the last five-plus years, but I have turned into a back-country travel-hungry maniac. Okay, maybe I do know what has happened. The kids are no longer kids—even though they will always be called The Kids. My husband will tell you that he thinks I have been in a midlife crisis since I was nineteen, always trying something new or taking unnecessary risks. As mid-40s reality settled in five years ago, the clock really feels like it is ticking loudly.

Since I became an adult, I have travelled, but with a proper rolling suitcase and a hotel booking in hand. I also didn't mind visiting a country twice. The last five-plus years I have been finding countries I have never been to before, that are a little off the grid, and then travelling in their most remote areas, without a Wifi connection. I find myself connected to my now filthy backpack, hiking remote mountain ranges and really finding connections with the people of the country. I literally crave getting to know the nature and people of each country.

Travelling opens up your world to how big our planet is; to how many cultures live so differently than yours; to different views on politics, philanthropy, and living. This type of life-thinking opens up your mind—and wide. New experiences and connections to people, landscapes, customs, traditions and daily life helps us understand this big 'ol world better.

One summer, my daughter and I travelled to Spain and Portugal. I wanted to teach her that you did not have to be rich to travel to beautiful places, but you could be resourceful. We learned from a website called workaway.info, that you could travel the world by barter exchanging your services such as waitressing, graphic design, construction, and many more. We excitedly signed up for cleaning rooms, gardening and cooking at a villa in Spain in exchange for accommodation.

The owner of the villa and myself set up a Skype call to get to know each other, just to make sure she was not an axe murderer. I think she was also doing the same. Julie was lovely, and she told me she has never had such a seasoned worker stay with her. Which really meant, someone as old as I was. However, this aging business worked for me, as she asked if we would be interested in house sitting versus working at her villa while she went on a vacation. Ummmm, yes! After driving the winding vineyard roads to a remote village in Spain, we arrived at her stunning villa at the top of the hill. The villa was in a gorgeous vineyard with rolling hills, beautiful horses, a friendly dog, a cat and an inviting pool. We learned how to live in a small Spanish village, eat their food, and enjoy the locals socially in the town square every night. We watched the family generations connect each day, working together in their butcher shop or playing cards on their front steps. Oh, and we learned how to take care of a huge Spanish villa. We truly immersed ourselves in their culture. A life-changing experience.

One summer, my son and I travelled to Japan. I wanted to teach him the rewards of backpacking from destination to destination on an ancient spiritual pilgrimage trail, called the Kumano Kodo. For over a week, we stayed in people's homes as we hiked this mountain range from village to village, sleeping and eating with families. Upon arriving at each remote village or passing by a rice field, the farmers always stopped to wave and welcome us. We slept in rooms with thin screens with little to no privacy; on the floors with thin mats and hard rice pillows. We ate the food that two or three proud "aunties" cooked for us each night, serving unique and exquisite dish after dish. We learned how to communicate without English. We took brave chances on what we were eating with the "aunties" standing over us, hoping we would enjoy the dishes they lovingly cooked. The "aunties" invited their neighbours to meet us and look at us, as in this remote region of Japan they don't see many North Americans. We experienced *sentos* and *onsens*, which are public baths or hot springs separated into male and female areas, where you would bath nude with the other guests. We spent time with a monk without speaking and tried to understand their spirituality through meditation. Another wonderful immersion into Japanese culture and living.

The travel journeys and stories like this are many and truly life changing. These experiences build our character for our life decisions and strength. I have learned so much with each country I explore. That being financially poor isn't always a sad thing when you have your family close and food you know how to gather from the water and land.

I have learned I can educate people across the world about how I live, to their great interest and awe, who have no idea where my country is on a world map or what a hockey stick is. I learned that we could reduce prejudice just by meeting people eye to eye, without understanding a word of each other's language. I have learned that your cup of coffee each morning has twenty-eight processes to go through before it reaches your mouth, and it starts with people climbing up muddy, scary jungle hills to get to the coffee bean plants.

I learned that a simple act of giving two days of my salary back to a village can put doors on homes that look like shacks and protect families from being flooded. I learned that I can bring simple joy to people by visiting the homeland they are proud of, as they learn how far I have come to see their country. I learned how we can make each other feel important.

I learned that travelling with my kids in remote parts of the world, seeing life outside their life bubble, is one of the greatest parenting rewards that I have experienced. I learned about seeing landscapes that look surreal and impossibly beautiful. That I can work extra hard to fund this "outside the bubble" experience and figure out innovative ways to travel, bartering my skills in exchange for accommodation.

I learned that I want to keep learning more and more outside my bubble; that it feels almost like an addiction—but a good one.

Now go get outside your bubble—the world is waiting to meet you.

THE *Stranger* CONNECTION

Why? Why not? I am famous—okay, not literally famous—for saying, "why not?" It seems to stop people in their tracks to do some quick calculations on the why nots. Usually there aren't that many why nots to justify not going for it. This is how I feel about connecting to strangers. Yes, I understand there are risks in having a stranger hop into a car with you or invited through the front door of your home. But if you don't take a chance on connecting to a stranger, you could miss out on some significant life awesomeness that connection can bring to you.

Can I truly say my life is richer and has reaped rewards from connecting with a stranger? Yes, 100%.

In my career days of fundraising for the needs of children and youth, I attended a philanthropy lunch with over two hundred non-profit leaders. The lunch invited charity leaders from around the city to listen to a keynote speaker and a topic that would keep inspiring us to raise funds. The speech was intended to remind us how valuable it is for people to make investments in our community, and our non-profits, so we can change our part of the world.

The speaker that day was Justin Trudeau, but he wasn't who made an impression on me. It was a man named, Alvin. Before Justin Trudeau came on stage, he was to be introduced by Alvin. The lights dimmed and a voice came across the speaker system, asking us to close our eyes. A few minutes later, we heard a wicked drum solo and opened our eyes to see who was hammering out this beat magic. Then we saw Alvin—with sweat dripping down his face, that scrunched-up drummer face expression—playing the drums with his feet, as he had no arms.

I felt a rush of energy I can only explain as connection. After the drum solo, Alvin came to the front of the stage to tell us he was born with no arms. His young birth mother didn't know how to parent him, so he was raised by a large foster family, who treated all the kids the same. Even with no arms, his dad expected him to mow the lawn and figure it out. He talked about great perseverance and that he was living proof that anything is possible; that obstacles can be removed if you truly want them to. I learned that labels don't need to exist.

After the lunch, I rushed to meet Alvin and tell him how he touched me and hoped he wouldn't think I was crazy with all my connection-feelings. To my relief he didn't, and we readily exchanged phone numbers. We stayed in contact for years, and he helped give hope to the work I was doing with kids in foster care and finding forever families. I will never forget his spirit.

Was the time invested getting to know a bit of someone put to good use and worth my time? Yes, 100%.

Being a city girl at heart, I had always worked in and around downtown. Moving to the 'burbs to raise kids with trees, a tire swing (that we have yet to put up) and a house we could afford to buy, seemed like a good plan. Driving downtown years ago from the 'burbs, would take forty-five minutes and at most, one hour. Once the rest of the world discovered our 'burb gem, the commute started to creep up. Once we had kids and still no tire swing, the commute was hitting one-and-a-half hours each way, minimum.

This became a problem when the kids hit twelve years old, could walk to school themselves and we were an hour-and-a-half away at work. Precisely at 3:30 pm was our daily after school check-in phone call: "I walked safely home, no I didn't get in a van with strangers for candy." Well, during one particular phone call check-in, I heard a lot of noise in the background. I asked the kids what the noise was all about and they explained they had invited about ten kids over to play. Holy moly. Ten kids in our yard unsupervised and running wild! I was about to dial 911 to move those kids along, as there was no way I could get back home in under two hours to do it myself. So, on that day, I decided to get a job out in the 'burbs and be close to home.

Except, I discovered there really wasn't any obvious career jobs in the 'burbs that aligned with my skills. I also discovered that I really didn't know a lot of my community that well, outside of school, the ball field and the ice arena. Plus, we coached all the sports and volunteered in the school, so really, I only knew twelve-year-old kids and a handful of parents.

I decided to do a one-woman campaign and let the 'burbs know I was looking for a job. One of the best ways to get to know people is to volunteer. I started to ignore the Vancouver Sun newspaper landing on my doorstep and started to read the local paper. Right in front of me, was a volunteer advertisement calling for a social planning advisory committee member for our city. I had no idea what that meant, but it sounded like somewhere I could get to know my 'burb better.

I still remember the day I went in for my volunteer interview. The meeting was at city hall, which I didn't have a clue where it was, where I met two passionate, local community leaders. Both were strangers to me. Listening to them both, I couldn't believe they cared so much for our 'burb. They grew up in the community, raised their families, and were deeply rooted to make positive change for future generations. I had never experienced or met local community leaders who were so dedicated, so loyal to their home.

I was in disbelief, in awe, and was sold on this 'burb community leadership business.

Mind DOODLES

Not only did I start volunteering with these two strangers who I now call friends, I also joined a local 'boot camp' as part of my, "I need a job in the 'burb" campaign. This wasn't just any boot camp with a whistle and camouflage fatigues, it was another example of a deeply rooted community, but this time, with fitness. I was in more disbelief and awe as I witnessed the boot camp leader, who also was deeply rooted in the 'burb, really care about her members. I saw the members, in turn, really care about each other. Who knew? A 'burb fitness family. More strangers and more connections. Everyone who heard and embraced my "I need a job in the 'burb" campaign, took it seriously. And then it happened.

One boot camp morning, after much 6:00 am groaning, we were tasked to do a warmup run. One of the inspiring community leaders joined me in the run. She told me about a 'burb career opportunity and that she thought I would be perfect for it. She was right.

What I didn't know then, was how those four strangers inspired me to change the next ten years of my life. I am now proud to be part of the 'burb community leadership ranks, with a legacy job and my own deeply rooted volunteer impact. Grateful and beyond, for these stranger connections.

Can you even really make a meaningful connection with someone you know in less than a day or a short period of time? Knowing that you most likely will never see them again in your life? Yes, 100%.

I have always loved to gourmet cook. Give me a dinner party menu to create or bring on the fancy hors d'oeuvres, and welcome to my taste-testing kitchen. I had never had formal chef training and thought it was time to dust off my bucket list by striking off a trip to a cooking school in Tuscany. I know, rough, right? I also wanted to do the trip on my own and practice my solo adventuring for inner reflection downtime.

When I told my friends of this solo adventuring plan, they all had a good laugh. You? Alone? That's a good one. They all knew me too well, where I can't just invite one person to the party, it has to be one hundred. I love people and I love being surrounded by them...all. My friends had a good point. So, I made a plan. I would strategically go to this cooking school with my head down and not do a lot of talking, so people would assume I was shy and introverted. I could do that—I would only have to last seven days—geesh.

Okay, I only lasted like ten minutes—well, maybe five minutes. I drove through the magnificent, tree-lined vineyard's rolling hills to the cooking school gate entrance that looked like a fairy tale on steroids. I was setting myself up for failure to not gush with excitement upon arrival. So, I threw away my solo adventure inner reflection downtime plan, stranger-connected in five minutes flat, and gushed.

I am so glad I ditched my pretending-to-be-shy plan. If I didn't, I might not have connected with my 'soul sister.' I am not sure how it all happened. Maybe it was her sassy sense of humour, maybe it was her willingness to have wine for breakfast or maybe it was her intellect—but I sure did stranger-connect. I met this young woman that I felt I had known all my life. I was drawn to her life story and to her shiny charisma. We spent that week together like sisters who planned this trip for months back home. We talked nonstop and life shared. We connected with the other guests and made our 'pack.' We cooked away in our fairy tale setting and were already feeling sad about saying goodbye.

We decided to not say goodbye so soon. Totally out of character, my new soul sister changed her travel plans and hopped in the car with me for another week of Tuscany fun. She typically was organized, liked a plan, and didn't stray from it. But this time she did, as our stranger connection was so strong. For me, this was great, I loved avoiding plans and being carefree. However, I did question the risk. What did I really know about this stranger, with the exception of a week of great conversation and laughter? Would she steal my cash? Would she become awful to travel with? Would she take advantage of me? Would she ruin my bucket list vacation?

I decided the risk was worth it as she was absolutely a hoot. Off we went, with tunes cranked, hitting the Tuscany roads less travelled. We adventured beautifully through backroad wineries and discovered hot springs to jump in down a bumpy, dirt road. We became Italian foodie champions, shopped leather markets with passion, and made historic memories together. This stranger-connection was meaningful in more ways than I can express. It was a beautiful human experience, connecting in that way, taking a chance on having a connection make a forever positive footprint on your heart. Thelma and Louise with no murder and a good ending. I am forever thankful.

My hope is that I have created stranger-connection curiosity, hope, contemplation and belief. I realize my stranger-connection story list could have been an entire book on its own. My wish is that you also have the same positive stranger-connection stories in abundance to share or will have throughout your life.

Just think: stranger-connection, why not?

Mentor LAND

I am goo goo ga ga over the value of mentorship. Don't bother googling "goo goo ga ga," as it really means, strongly believing. For me, having a mentor, aka being a mentee, means that I can draw upon that person's lived experience and their knowledge. I can count on and trust that person to have my back and steer me in the right direction. You could have a mentor for a specific thing like a work expertise or a relationship skill. A mentor can also be a generalist, someone you greatly admire and respect their opinion or way of life.

Being a mentor is an honour and extremely gratifying. Having someone to look up to you, and knowing they rely on you, is a great life reward. Being a mentor can give you a powerful purpose. The mentor and mentee relationship doesn't have to be life-long, it can be short lived and have a short purpose. Whether long or short, it is a positive impact on both lives. Mentorship touches my life constantly—I welcome it fully and completely.

Most of my friends and my work colleagues have been instant mentors in my life, whether they are formally aware of it or not. My friendships are unique and diverse, and I get to sponge up all their life expertise, regularly. I lean into each of my friend's strengths and life journeys to build and guide my own. Through work, I have been surrounded by the smartest people with an enormous amount of talent. Every colleague has given me nuggets of knowledge, leadership style and skills that I throw into my own foundation, allowing me to direct and guide organizations to where they want to go.

I love being a mentee. Allowing ourselves to be in an open space and be curious is very fulfilling. To be able to ask questions that may not come across as very dazzling, and to simply learn from another human being with no cost but time, gives me a huge rush. Does it get better than that? Okay, don't answer that. I have never experienced anyone saying no to me when I have asked for their mentorship. I find, people appreciate the mentorship request and the experience.

When I was getting into my fundraising career after my first two careers in accounting and then technology, I realized I didn't really know what I was getting myself into. So, I set out to find myself a mentor. I researched all the charities I thought did an excellent job at fundraising, picked my top charity, and made a phone call to a director named Janice. Janice didn't miss a beat when I asked her for mentorship, and she invited me to her office the next day. I learned a lot from Janice over a couple of years. She generously shared her style, her learnings, and her talent with me. This mentorship experience gave me confidence to be a kick-ass fundraiser. In turn, I became a mentor to other fundraisers through the fundraising association—always keeping Janice's mentorship generosity top of mind.

At another stage of my fundraising career, I worked for an organization that focussed on the world of adoption. This charity did outstanding work, but outside their inner circle, no one knew about the difference they were making for children. I searched for a mentor that could get this organization recognized and on the map. I met Fred, who I knew was a media dynamo, at a coffee shop on Commercial Drive in Vancouver, who agreed to be my mentor and take on this big awareness challenge. Fred took on this mentorship role fearlessly and successfully, encouraging thousands of people to support adoption. Fred showed me that high energy mixed with determination can move mountains, and Fred, the dynamo, sure did.

Even at the seasoned stages of my career, I continually need mentorship.

I started working in a community where I did not have many business development connections. I was at the gym one day (there seems to be a common theme of me meeting people while sweating) and I met this firecracker of a lady named Jan. She and I hit it off instantly. She was cheeky, smart and super funny. As I got to know Jan over push ups, I learned she was a top realtor and on every Board of Directors in town. I asked her if she would become my mentor in the community and take me under her wing to show me around. Jan, just like Janice, didn't miss a beat. We went out for a drink a few days later to figure out how she could help. She took me to every networking event in the community, introducing me to her friends and family. Not only did Jan mentor me to become a community leader, she also became a good friend, a big sister type, I will always look up to.

I also love being a mentor. I get to take all my life learnings from myself, my family, friends and mentors, and dump them in a big pile to offer up to my mentee. It really is a true 'pay it forward' concept.

I had always had a passion to become a Big Sister mentor. When I hit twenty-something, I was ready, and became a Big Sister mentor of the Big Brothers Big Sisters charitable organization. This has been one of my life's greatest gifts.

I met Melissa when she was seven years old. Bright baby-blue eyes, unruly blond hair full of curls and a shy dimply smile that melted your heart. If love at first sight with a seven-year-old can happen, it did to me that day. Her mom wanted Melissa to have more life experiences and felt a Big Sister mentor would be the way. I was a perfect match, since I was more than game to share any life experience I could—especially with this adorable kid! We went fishing, to plays, ice skating, biking, hiking and bowling. We did crafts, we did homework, baked

Mind DOODLES

cookies, went on rollercoasters and watched a million movies. You name the fun activity, we did it.

As Melissa got older, I could tell that one of her favourite activities was coming grocery shopping with me and learning how to make dinner. Are you kidding? No, this was not a joke. Melissa was enjoying being mentored in domestic life. Who knew? This was when our relationship went from mentorship to real sisterhood. Melissa became part of my family. One of the biggest honours in my life was when Melissa's mom asked if she could name me in her will to look after both of her daughters if she died when they were still young. Not only did I get a little sister, but I also got an extended family. Melissa has also become a big sister to my kids. Driving them places, giving them advice and simply being part of our family. My husband also has a very soft spot for Melissa and always nudges me to check in on her.

Today, Melissa is getting ready to graduate as a Psychiatric Nurse. I am excited I get to host her grad dinner around our dining room table, where she sits at with every family holiday and celebration. The life reward that Melissa has given me is hard to define, as she is part of my heart. I am one proud Big Sister. I am one proud mentor.

Go goo goo ga ga over mentorship and open your arms to catch all the life rewards.

THOUGHT
Shoot Out

I believe I shared earlier, that it turns out I only have a writing short game in me. I have no patience for the long writing game (not enough constant action)—thus no romantic fiction novel production. Yes, I know you are relieved.

In devotion to the writing short game, I am sharing snippets of random thoughts and well, I guess, the leftovers of what I know.

Enjoy the "thought shoot out" read.

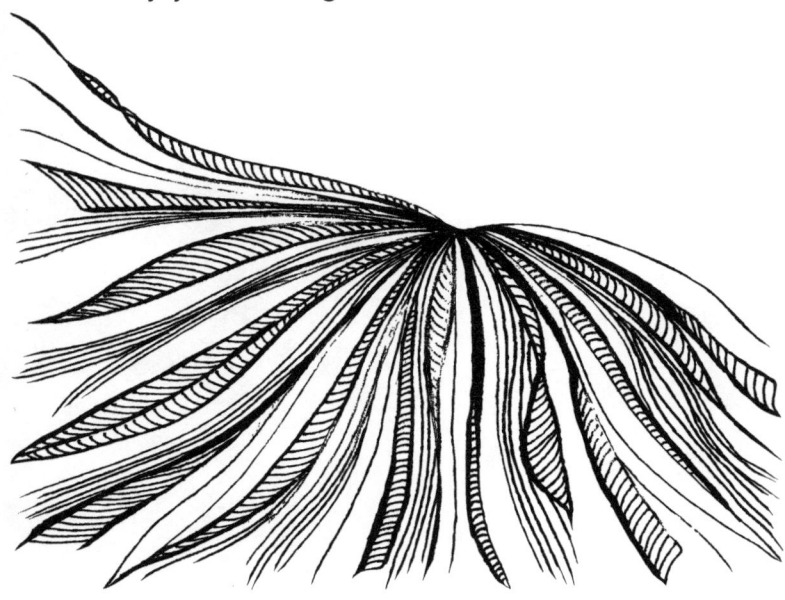

1970s Babes

This book would not be complete if I did not do a walk down memory lane for all of us 1970s babes—thanks Lori for letting me steal your fabulous title, you 1970s babe, you! We babes grew up in an era where our moms still embraced the 1950s housewife personality. Or alternatively, they were already empowered from the Women's Movement, with breaking free from it, with careers, and "I am woman, hear me roar" yelling.

Personally, I would have loved to have been part of this Women's Movement shift. Born twenty years too late. Oh, and I would have loved bellbottoms and being a hippie. I think I would have been a great hippie. A hippie and a bold career—a winning combo.

We grew up with cigarettes and station wagons with no seatbelt laws. We wore shirts with big colourful rainbows on the front, from sleeve to sleeve. Most of us only had one channel on our TVs that we had to physically turn on/off and rabbit ears we had to adjust to get rid of the TV screen fuzz. We saw our moms watch the soap opera, "Edge of Night," religiously each day on that one channel, where talking was forbidden during that hour.

We talked on rotary phones that hurt our fingers from all the dialing. We also had to deal with party lines—yes, you had to share a phone line with your neighbours, and then we moved to experiencing busy signals. We ate masses of food in plastic: hot dog wieners, Kraft cheese slices and Twinkies. We drank pop from the Pop Shoppe, orange, grape and root beer. We went to drive-ins to watch movies or have a milkshake. We put hockey cards in our bike spokes to hear the card-clicking for entertainment as we sped down a hill on our banana seat. We loved marble day at school as a highlight, where we knocked down and traded "steelies" or "cat's eyes."

We had sports days, with jugs of McDonald's orange drink and ribbons that clearly marked winners along with losers. We had the first Atari video game unit that played Pong with two lines and a circle—for less than superior graphics. We played records upon records of Fleetwood Mac and Motley Crew. We played 45s upon 45s of Prince and Madonna. We played in "air bands," went to arcades and danced at soc hops (yup, in our socks). We loved our Slinkies, Rubik's Cubes and Cabbage Patch Dolls. We watched *Happy Days*, *Gilligan's Island* and *Three's Company* on TV.

We listened to our very own home-made mixed music cassette tapes on "ghetto blasters" on our shoulders, walking down the street. We then walked down the streets with Walkmans in our ears, having to unjam the tape ribbon half the time. We wore thick, canvas, acid wash, tightest-as-you-can-get-'em-pulling-them-up-with-a-hanger, Levis jeans. Then we moved on to the more stylish, French cut jeans. We wore long flowery skirts and jean jackets with our fairy boots or gel shoes.

We wore gigantic scrunchies in our hair in a side ponytail. We loved banana clips in our hair and thick gooey lip gloss called Kissing Potion. We roller-skated on Friday nights with our yellow or red satin jackets and matching hats. During the day we sat on sunny decks with our baby oil to speed up the tan, Sun-In hair spray to be blonder, and Quick Tan that turned our skin orange. We passed around thousands of doodle notes in the school classroom to our friends. We learned how to talk "Valley Girl."

We hung out at 7-Eleven on Saturday nights with our Coke Slurpees and talked to cute boys with their collars flipped up. We met at the gas station to leave our notes, describing where the party was that night. All as a way to communicate with each other—nope, no cell phone, texting, snapping or tic-tocking. We were the era of the biggest hair with hairspray that made it rock hard, the Mullet, parachute pants, head bands, big waist belts, bigger hip belts, leg warmers and gigantic glasses. Note: all of those have made a comeback at least a few times, with the exception of one—where the heck is the big hair? I am waiting.

THIS IS WHAT I KNOW

Crossing
YOUR FUN LINE

We have all been victim to crossing the Fun Line. Or we may have been very close to that line, just teetering over the edge. I absolutely know the line well, seems so fun! I warn you it is not. Every time my kids go out, I say, "Know your Fun Line"—which is code for don't get too drunk. Ha, and now that I think of it, I say it to my husband too. The Fun Line is for all ages, 19+, of course.

It takes a lot of discipline and hard work to know your line.

You must have a watch handy and monitor the cocktail-intake timing when the night moves speedy fast. You must make sure you have a food base in your stomach of just the right carbs. You have to make sure you drink lots of water and try to follow the 'ol one alcohol drink to one glass of water, system. Let me tell you, this one sets you up for failure every time—who can really keep track? And if you can keep track, are you really even close to your Fun Line?

You also have to consider the "out of nowhere" surprise shots of *Jägerbombs* or the chilled espresso Van Gogh vodka arrival, followed by that yucky pickle juice shot. Mix this with peer pressure—which I am absolutely guilty as charged—and that line comes creeping closer and closer.

Knowing how to stay on the good side of the line takes awareness, skill and experience. If you cross your line, there is no going back. You will get attacked by the spins, the sweats, the vomits and the inability to walk or speak. Night and fun game over. You just have to hope your wing man or woman has not crossed their line too, or your mom isn't looking at her own Fun Line, so someone can get you home safely.

Words to live by: Know your Fun Line.

Decade MANIA

I am not going to spend too much time whining about turning fifty. I am just going to spend a moment or two on the whine. Stay with me. I don't know about you—yes, I am speaking to anyone over forty-five, but when I pass by a mirror I say, "Hey, who is that?" Seriously, my body does not match my brain. I don't think I'm in a time warp, but inside, I'm definitely aging slowly. Outside, not so much.

Feeling twenty-five and thinking I'm twenty-five, literally surprises me when I look in my rearview mirror while I am driving. It only takes a few seconds for the shock to wear off and no, it does not happen every time, but it happens enough to remind me that I feel half my age inside.

I also get "age reminded" when I am out and about. My favourite one was when my friends and I went to a nightclub downtown to enjoy dancing at 80s night. Here we were, shaking our booty to Bon Jovi's "Livin' On A Prayer," and these twenty-year-olds came up to us and say, "Good for you!"

Are you freaking kidding me?

This was our era, our tunes, our hot 80s guy, and you say, good for us? These types of "age reminders" don't stop on the dance floor. It happens every time I go grocery shopping and the cute young bagging dude says, "Do you want help carrying your bags to your car?" and then he throws in a "ma'am."

Are you freaking kidding me?

Mind DOODLES

I could bench-press three times the weight of the grocery bags I got here, throw you in the mix and still be fine. And let's change that "ma'am" to "babe" or "chick"—shall we?

That's enough on the whine, as I know I am-over-the-moon lucky to have made it to this age and can whine about all these "freaking kidding me's." I know every decade has its "thing," and it's different for everyone. Let's work backwards and start with forty.

Aww forty. Many say life starts at forty. Or forty is the new thirty. Or is that forty, is the new black? Or orange? It's hard to keep up. Forty seems to represent the age that you may experience a little family or life freedom. I have seen forty be the age where people reach their all-time career highs. Really, forty on average, could be your halfway point in life. I have heard this is the age where you really truly start to not care what people think of you—that sure sounds like a big relief. I have seen fabulous, fit and forty—the age where you start focussing on your health and wellness. I have heard this is also where a fabulous, fit and sex-life may escalate to new levels! Also expect to get reading glasses after you hit forty—wow, I think that was my first practical tip of this book.

Hello thirty! For me, this was the decade I had to grow up. I know you are thinking that doesn't make sense, as it doesn't seem like I'm that grown up right now. Well, can you imagine me pre-thirty? Oh yeah, wild and free! A lot of people start discovering themselves at thirty. They get their clearer direction on life, which is where that grown-up part may come in. This is a great entry point for responsibility, with a mortgage, career, family, marriage, or whatever big stuff you want to take on. I see people really start exploring at thirty and trying new stuff. New hobbies, new friend circles and new careers. At thirty it could mean progress, personal development and figuring out how to be you, as a grown-up. Personally, I wasn't be a big fan of thirty.

Three cheers for twenty! I say, time to bust all out in this decade. Enjoy ten years of no responsibility except putting yourself through education and getting a career start at the mid to tale-end of twenty. This is your time to just go for it. Senseless road trips, find your fun pals, do ridiculous things and chalk it up to life learning. It is the decade to find your independence. Learn who you like and what you like. Do what you want, when you want. Learn to like yourself, even love yourself. Figure out your passions and go explore this bad-ass world. Enjoy being the young'un wherever you go, before you aren't. Welcome, no one bossing you around except yourself. Doesn't this sound amazing? Yup, you can see why I am stuck at twenty-five. Three more cheers for twenty!

If we are fortunate enough, we all take a turn at Decade Mania, but know you always get to relish your real age inside—just watch those mirrors.

PARENT
Joy Ride

I am pretty sure there are hundreds of thousands of books and lectures on parenting. So, I'm going to try to high-level it in one short rant. Get ready for the most fun, grinding, sad, happy, joyful, upset, crazy, back to happy again—ride of your life…and with the parent joy ride, expect everything and expect nothing.

Get ready for your heart to burst through your body with out-of-control love you never knew was possible. Get ready to turn into a bear—like, really a bear, like *Mama Bears and Papa Bears Gone Wild*—I'm sure it's a blockbuster movie somewhere. The bearlike tendencies just happen out of nowhere and you may have no control. With this knowledge, you might as well get rid of any parental judgement you may have before you begin. Develop big shoulders to stand up to any asshole that may decide to judge you as a parent. Seriously, every kid is different, every parent is different, and every family makeup is different—don't let judgement take you down. What do they know?

Definitely expect to turn into a crazy person now and then, as that type of earth-shattering love can make the sanest of us, a little cuckoo. If you are a good person, with strong values, integrity, ethics, and an open mind, you will be an awesome parent. You are going to make a zillion mistakes—yes, that is a number, and yes, that is how many mistakes you will make, just learn from them and move on.

You need to be able to reach out and ask for help—continually. You will be surrounded by people who have been great parents and who will be happy to share their zillion mistakes—learn from them. There are experts out there, like counsellors and therapists who can help, and you may need to be courageous enough to just reach out. Sometimes, parents hide behind closed doors with their parenting fears or shame. Sometimes those parents look freshly put together and sometimes they don't. Not everyone will talk about their parenting woes, but you should and encourage others to as well.

Oh, and you should know you will need to consider stopping swearing, smoking pot, cheating at card games, rule breaking and being hungover, if you want to be any kind of good role model. Or alternatively, hide it well—ha!

I think you can read all you want on being the best parent. I think you can analyze, strive and dream about what type of parent you would like to be. I think you can look at parents you admire or your own parents and take the best-of-the-best from them. I think when you begin your parenting journey, it leads you, not the other way around.

I believe parenting is one of those things you don't know until you know. It feels like a continual work in progress. Your child will develop, change, demand and grow, constantly. Your parent job is to keep them safe, keep them nurtured, be their life teacher, life guide and love them to pieces. You will have immensely proud moments and you will have deflated disappointing ones. You will feel elated at times and other times feel in survival mode. You could feel in control one minute and the next minute feel helpless.

That is all part of the Parent Joy Ride. Yipeeeeee.

Oh, and you may become really, really, really tired from all the bumps. Just know that is normal and there's nothing wrong with a quick power nap in your car in the parking lot if you need it.

From babies to toddlers to school-age to teenagers to young adults. The Parent Joy Ride is one over-the-top journey. I always find it helpful to keep the big picture in mind, whatever that is for you. For me, it is raising my kids to be thoughtful, independent, happy, strong, contributing members in society, whatever that looks like for them. Whether you raise a kid that never passes a piece of litter on the side of the road without picking it up or a kid that grows up to be a cancer researcher—it all counts and matters.

If you choose not to become a parent, that works too. You can contribute and help other parents raise great kids. There are loads of them around.

Hang on and enjoy the ride.

NATURAL *Highs*

One of the best stories that went down in my life was at my forty-ninth birthday last year. Each birthday I try to find new, unique, wild and fun birthday adventures to top the last one. My friends, who are the very best, wait in anticipation for the birthday adventure invite, and off we go. They let me plan everything and simply ask me how much they owe for their travel-cost portion. Again, they are the very best.

Last year I decided to hit one of the San Juan Islands and stay in this fancy shmancy world renowned oceanfront hotel. The location and resort had been on my bucket list for awhile and I was very excited to hit the "book" button on Travelocity. After work on a Friday, I raced in my apple-red Dodge Charger to pick up my pals, get through the US border, stop at duty free and make one of the last ferries of the night to the islands.

On the ferry, the girls broke out the red cups and were enjoying a few boat bevvies. Being the driver, I drank water and was dreaming of my first lemon drop martini upon arrival. After eight hours of travel, the GPS announced we were a few minutes away from the prestigious hotel. My friends decided it was a good idea to treat me to a 21-year-old birthday tiara to honour my celebration and threw this adorable gold crown on my head before we checked in.

The hotel did not disappoint; it was grand, luxurious and gorgeous. Like a pack of teenage girls, we ran to the front doors, checked in with the front desk clerk (who cheerily sang a welcome song to us) and raced to the lounge before they stopped serving dinner at 9:00 pm.

The lounge was full of boaters and happy laughing guests with live music playing. We quickly ordered our dinner and cocktails with the waiter who seemed to enjoy flirting with us—a bonus for the night! We each took a turn checking out the stunning outdoor pool overlooking the ocean and the rest of the dining space. We were so happy to be there. I was giddy and so thrilled to be celebrating my forty-ninth birthday with my best friends at a hotel I dreamed of staying at, for three entire sleeps.

Apparently, the flirting waiter thought I was too giddy, because when I went to order my second martini, he told me I was being cut off from any alcoholic beverage order but was happy to serve me water or coffee. Thinking this was a birthday joke, I started to have fun with this 'fake' cut off. However, the flirting waiter was no longer flirting and told me he was going to get his manager.

Ummmmm?

I went from flying high with happiness to dark reality. The manager told me that the servers and bar staff made a decision to stop serving me. You see, they thought I walked in the front doors of this esteemed hotel already intoxicated. They made an additional judgement call after my first martini, that I indeed was being overserved and for my own safety, decided to cut me off.

Now the point of the story is not how I lost my marbles to this accusation. Or how angry I was to be disregarded in this way on my very special forty-ninth birthday celebration. Or the revenge I took on this snooty hotel. That is a story to tell you about in person. The point of the story is about being naturally high on life and having people misinterpret that for being gunned.

Since when does being high on life turn into being too wasted? I have more questions than answers on this one. Was it the gold tiara that threw them off? Was it me acting twenty-five? Was it simply the bouncy chatter and the hyper excitement they don't typically see from a sober human being?

If being naturally high is a crime, then handcuff me. Well, maybe not, as that probably was the flirting waiter's next step to get me to leave their fine establishment—ha! My point is, always be naturally high.

Let 'er rip. Do you! Be you. Don't hold back. Clearly, we need more natural highs to pop up in this world.

Maybe we need more of the natural-high behaviour in this world to normalize it? To have natural highs be accepted. To be recognized and appreciated. Please join me in the Natural High Club. All sober, happy, playful, high-spirited members who like to life-celebrate with a little cray cray, are welcome.

ABOUT THE *author*

TREENA INNES is a first-time author who boldly jumped into writing her inaugural book head-first. She brings to her writing a unique lens on living a life that is action packed and what it all really means to her. With her trademark curiosity and mind that sparks with vision, she contributes professionally to working with organizations that are creating positive change. Passionate about adventures, she spends her time exploring life with her family and friends.

www.ingramcontent.com/pod-product-compliance
Lightning Source LLC
Chambersburg PA
CBHW050913160426
43194CB00011B/2395